Welcome to yOur Backyard

yOur Backyard Magazine, part of yourbackyard.us; a bi-monthly online and print "on demand" publication, encourages writers, actors, artists, musicians, photographers, gardeners, crafters, and youth [of all ages]. We also offer contests with the potential to be included in forthcoming issues of yOur Backyard Magazine and yOur Backyard books.

For each bi-monthly issue, we consider:

- Personal inspirational stories
- Poems
- Artwork
- Songs
- Photographs
- Biblical facts and/or applications

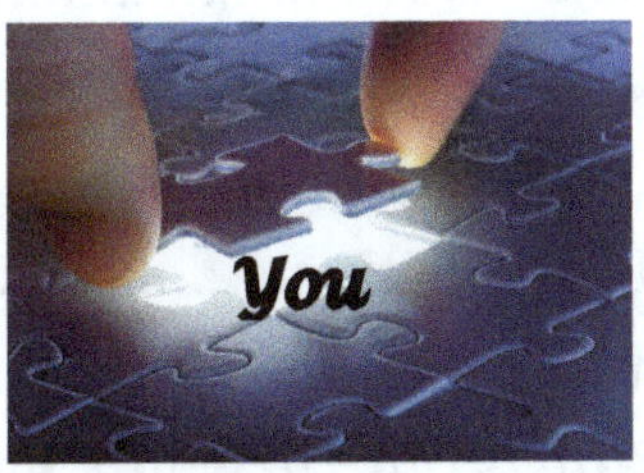

yOur Backyard, based on Luke 14:23, appreciates prayer.

**And the lord said unto the servant,
Go out into the highways and hedges,
and compel them to come in,
that my house may be filled.**

shELAH, editor and publisher
yOur Backyard Magazine

We look forward to hearing from you...

In this Issue...

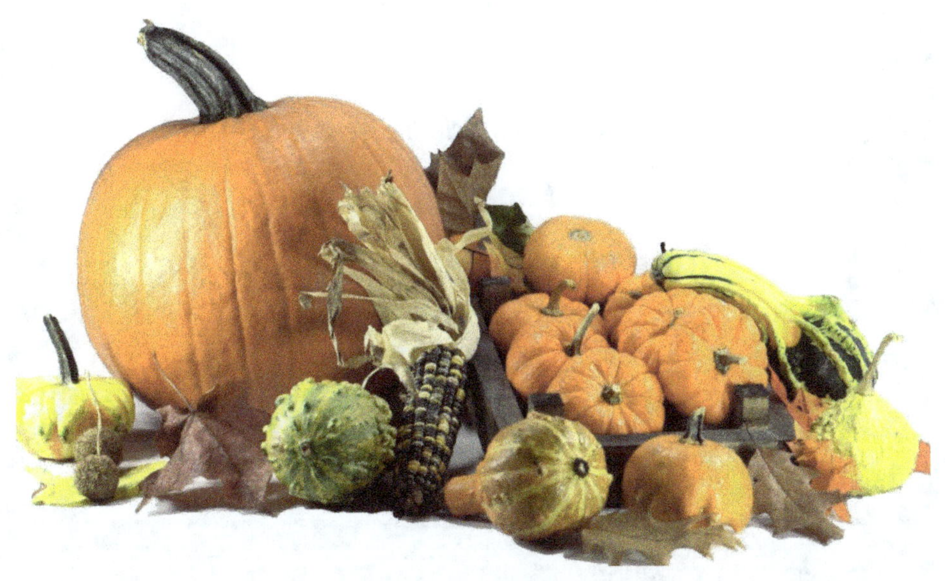

O give thanks unto the Lord;
call upon his name:
make known his deeds among the people.
~ Psalm 105:1

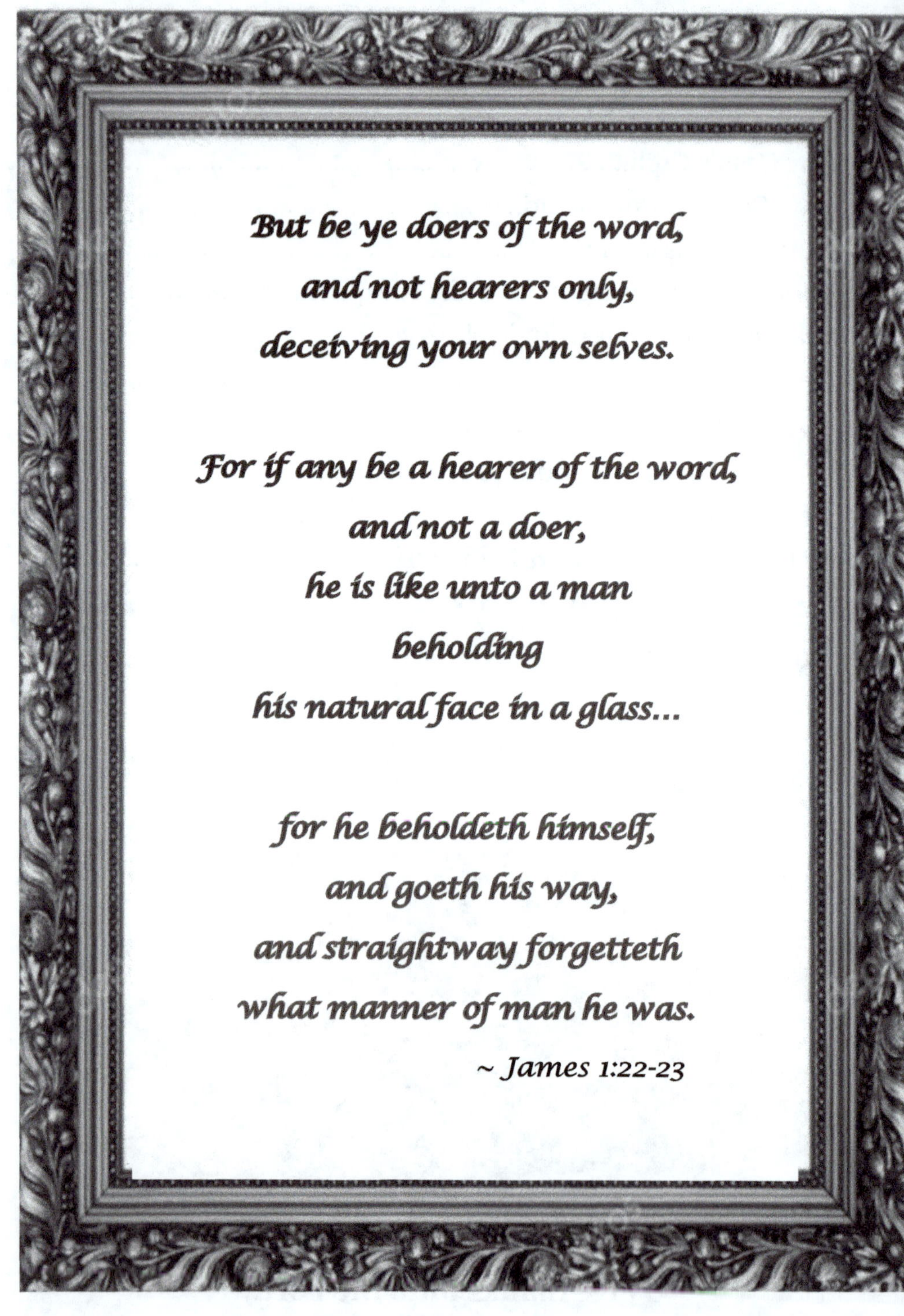

But be ye doers of the word,
and not hearers only,
deceiving your own selves.

For if any be a hearer of the word,
and not a doer,
he is like unto a man
beholding
his natural face in a glass...

for he beholdeth himself,
and goeth his way,
and straightway forgetteth
what manner of man he was.
~ James 1:22-23

Life Reflections...

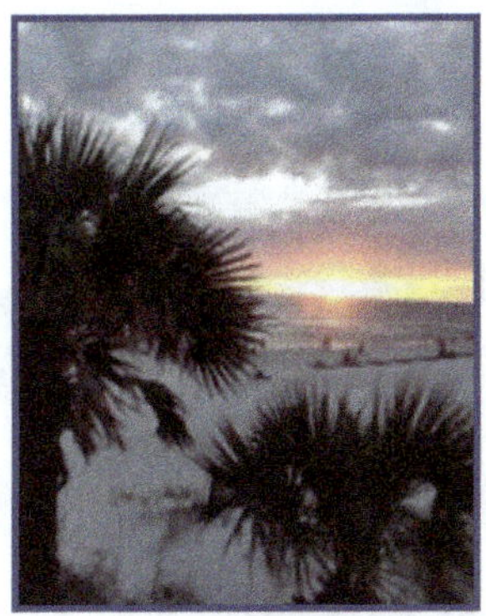

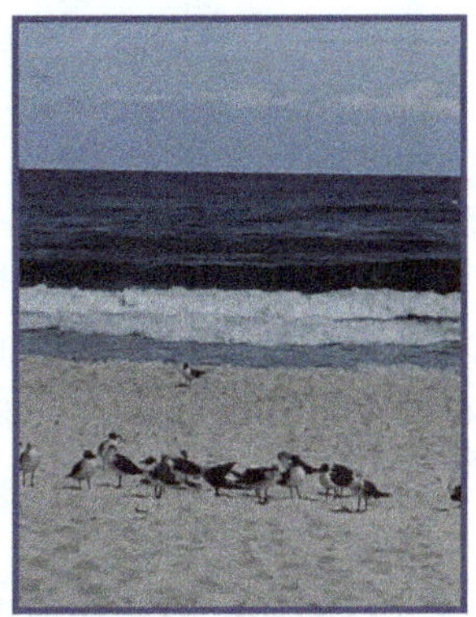

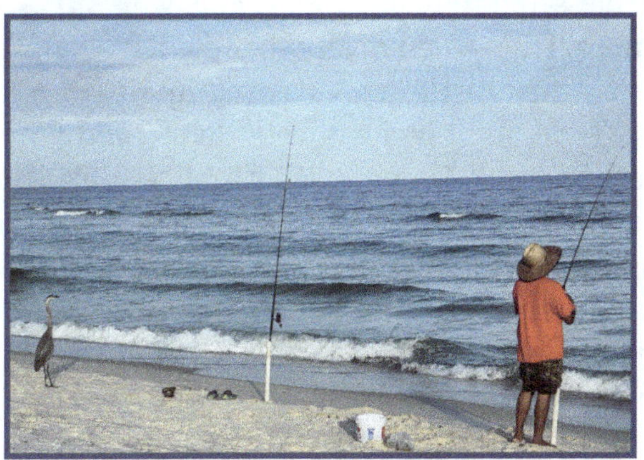

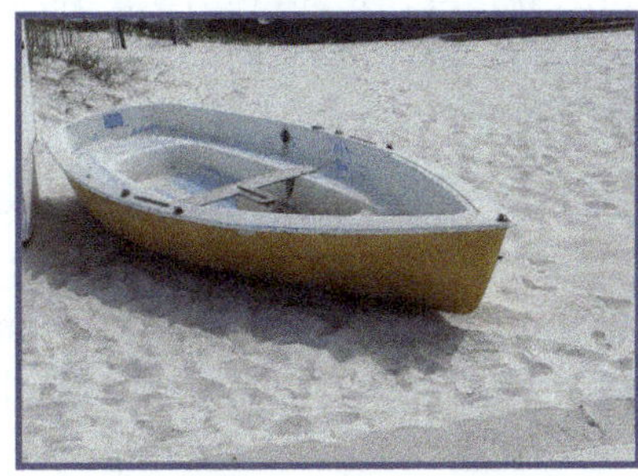

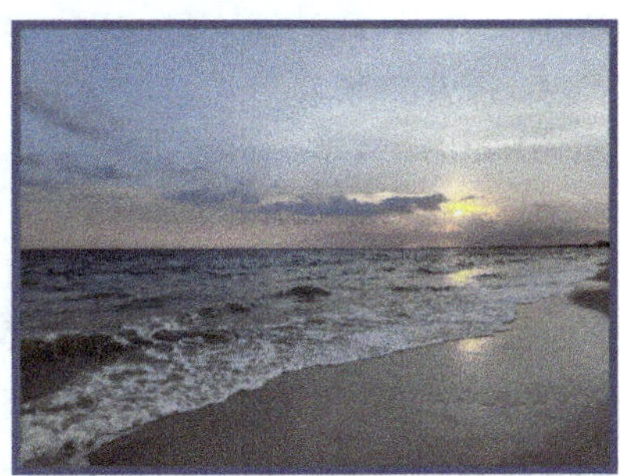

Amazing that the Lord:

> **...placed the sand for the bound of the sea
> by a perpetual decree, that it cannot pass it:
> and though the waves thereof toss themselves,
> yet can they not prevail; though they roar,
> yet can they not pass over it...**
>
> **~ Jeremiah 5:22**

My Perfect Imperfect Dolls
by
Mother as told to shELAH

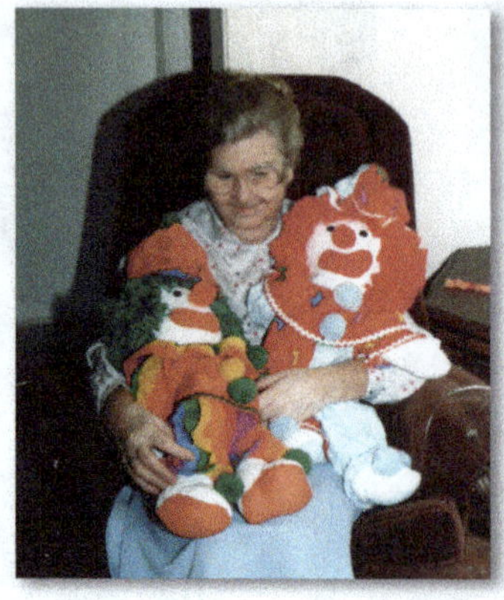

Because I am legally blind from retinitis pigmentosa, the dolls I create are not quite perfect. Each stitch, however, I sew with love. As I carefully shape doll hair from various yarn and fashion colorful clothes, I pray for those who will receive them.

Every so often, I remember times did not always seem so blessed. I remember long, lonely days and torrents of tears when my mother died the day after my third birthday. Growing up in the thirties, Gene, my black-haired, dark-eyed youngest brother became my best friend. We spent seemingly endless hours together; working on the farm; riding our horses, Dolly, and Maude.

Each spring, amidst the fragrance of blooming wildflowers, we picked blackberries and dewberries to be canned. "Watch out for snakes," Edlee, my oldest sister, warned. "Gene, you help Joy watch out, you know she doesn't see very well."

Armed with a jumbo stick, we nervously beat thick thorny berry bushes to scare away rattlesnakes that might lurk underneath. We swatted gnats, horseflies and pesky yellow jackets swarming around our sweaty faces. By the time we filled our buckets with juicy berries, our stomachs were also full.

Each day, we milked cows and gently lowered the milk jug, secured to a rope, down our well to keep it cool. At day's end, we gathered eggs from hen's hay feathered nests for tomorrow's breakfast. Often, when darkness fell, we chased fireflies and put them in jars. We ate parched peanuts from the hayloft stash as we listened to our battery powered radio. Sometimes, we burned "cow piles" to smoke away pesky mosquitoes that interrupted our sleep.

Usually, we only had enough money for basic necessities. Each winter, however, Gene and I anxiously awaited the time of year we expected to receive something special for Christmas. Gene wanted a toy log truck like the ones that hauled loads of pine trees to the nearby sawmill. I had my heart set on one toy I vowed to love and cherish —a Shirley Temple doll.

One summer day, Gene rushed up to me, grinning and showed me the toy log truck he had made. "What do you think, Sis?" he asked.

Later, I thought, if my brothers could make a truck, surely I could fashion a doll out of something. A pine log would be too rough, I decided. A dried ear of corn... no. What then?

A cucumber will be perfect for a doll's body, I thought, hurrying over to the field. When I reached the cucumber patch, I searched until I found one about a foot long, ripened into a pale yellow but still firm. Why stop with one doll? I thought. Why not make a daddy doll and baby as well?

With great care, I picked "perfect" bodies for my dolls. Slender long sticks doubled as legs, shorter twigs made tiny arms. With other bits and pieces of fallen twigs, I completed my cucumber babies with eyes, noses, ears and mouths. My cucumber doll family was not even remotely pretty. As I cared for each one, however, they, in a sense, fulfilled my desire for Shirley. Years later, one chilly Christmas morning I felt I must be dreaming. At last, I had my Shirley. The elegantly dressed doll with spirited brown eyes, tiny chestnut ringlets and an impish smile was mine, all mine.

I treasured Shirley for many years as I treated her like a guest when she visited my playhouse. The cucumber dolls I remade each year, on the other hand, ran the house. Unlike Shirley, they were family.

All my dolls vanished with days of my childhood. Memories, however, often come to mind as I sew. Today, I pray that those who receive my not-so-perfect dolls remember, even though we are not perfect— God loves each of us.

**Don't wait 'til I'm dead and gone to give me no flowers.
I want my roses while I'm living.**
~ Mother

Excerpt from *Roses for the Living* (Book available soon)

The Courage to Open Up

Brennan Clarneau

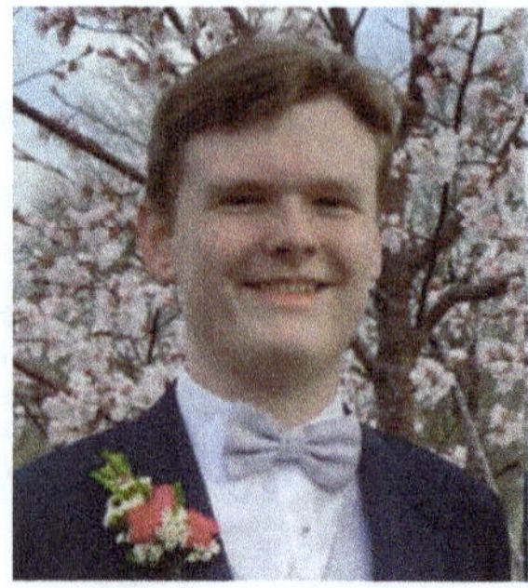

In the musical, "All Shook Up," I, **Brennan Daniel Clarneau**, a self-described Tennessee native, Christian, Conservative, Pro-lifer, Theater Nerd, play one of the lead actors. That character, Dennis, a nerdy, awkward high school student, aspires to be a dentist. He also struggles in communicating with girls, especially his "crush," Natalie.

Dennis repeatedly tries to let Natalie know that he likes her and would like to be her boyfriend. He repeatedly fails to follow through with letting Natalie know how he feels, however, and it becomes even more difficult when the cool biker-dude, Chad, comes to town and competes for Natalie's attention.

Dennis admires Chad, yet all the while being jealous of his attention to Natalie. By the end of the final act of "All Shook Up," Dennis finally gathers his courage to open up to Natalie. In turn, although Natalie rejects Dennis as her boyfriend, she and Dennis become real friends.

From stepping out of his comfort zone and sharing his feelings with Natalie, Dennis grows more confident in who he is as a person. He understands the value of friendship.

Acting on stage as well as behind the scenes, I've been involved in theater since the age of 10, with my first role in a play at church. Being in theater is one of the many ways God has actually used me to glorify Him and show my love for others. It has encouraged me to step out of my comfort zone and allowed me to make many friends that I likely would not have met otherwise.

I encourage others to participate in theater because it may do for them what it did for me:

- personally got me out of my comfort zone,

- allowed me to make several friends,

- provided a great way for me to socialize with others behind the scenes.

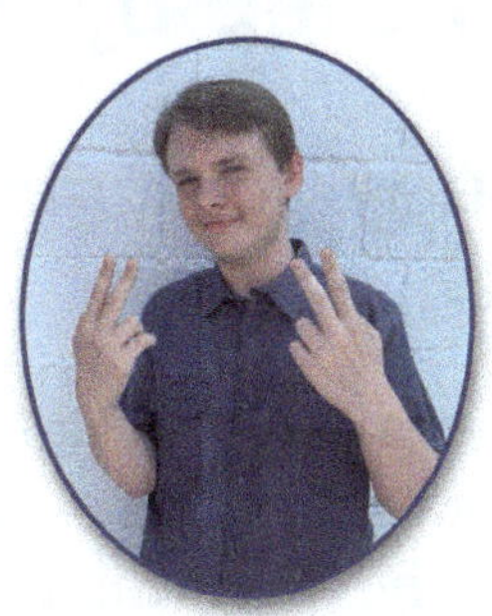

In theater, God has regularly given me opportunities to share my faith with fellow actors as well as those who work behind the scenes. During each production, I pray for those who do not know Jesus, both on and off stage, that they would personally know and believe in Him. I appreciate friends I've made and look forward to new ones I will make. My favorite Bible verse, Proverbs 27:17, states "As iron sharpens iron so one person sharpens another." I want to "sharpen" other people, to encourage them.

God called me to help embolden and build up others. Acting on stage as well as working behind the scenes in theater gives me opportunities to support my brothers and sisters in Christ. I can also pray for others to believe in and come to know Jesus as their personal Savior.

Addendum:

Although theater has been close to my heart and a major focus of my life for years, God has recently been telling me that at this time, it is not meant to be such a large part of my life. I thank those involved in theater with me... for being in my life. I love each of you. Remember also, that God loves you.

Goodbye theater... at least for now.

- Your friend, Brennan

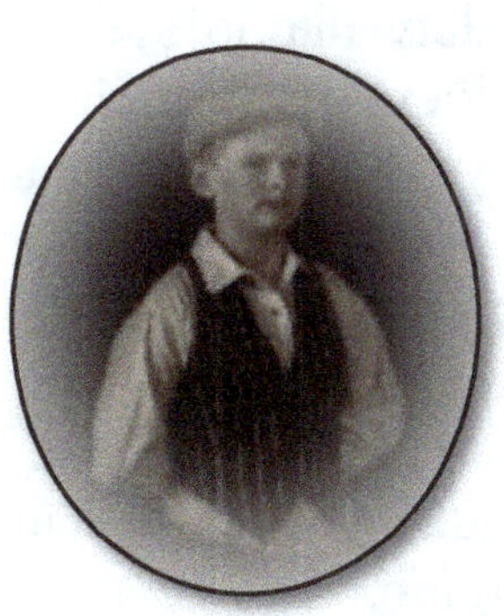

Step by Step by Step….
by
Sissy Scroggins

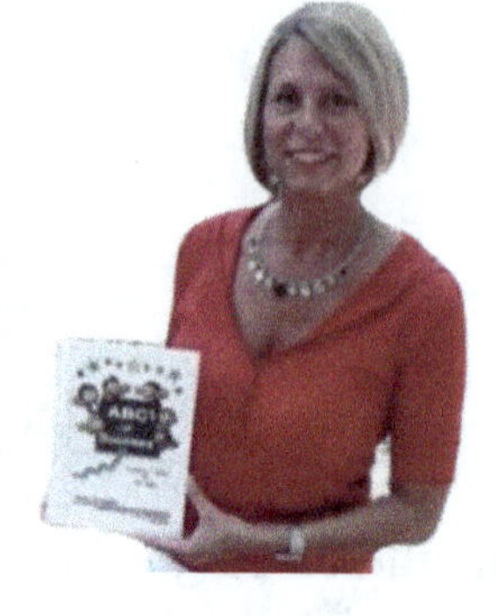

"Just take that first step…"

When Taylor, a younger friend told me, "I want to write a cookbook but there are so many cookbooks out there already…," I smiled and encouraged her to do it, to "just take that first step and start writing."

Instead of considering that thought, Taylor countered it with a frigid, faint-hearted frown.

"Why—what would be the use?" she asked.

"What if other cookbook authors thought that way?" I asked with a teasing "how dare you" look. "If more writers thought like you, we wouldn't have many books to read, would we, Taylor? And… last time I checked, **Amazon** did not feature any cookbooks by you on its website.

"What if artists thought they should not paint because the world already has too many works of art? Everything has been done under the sun—but not by you."

I tell others thinking about writing, painting, or tackling any creative art to take that first step. That one step will lead to another step, then another, and another…"

In writing, just as in painting or any other challenging pursuits in life, that first step, one of the hardest, requires that you set aside time to write. Then you write, write, write during that time. Israelmore Ayivor, an inspirational writer, and LifeSkills entrepreneur, said:

> The most difficult step ever is the first step.
> It comes with doubts, uncertainties, and all sort of fears.
> If you defy all odd[s] and take it,
> your confidence will replicate very fast
> and you'll become a master!

Mastering that first step naturally leads to the next one and then another and another and another. Years ago, when Zachary, my son, (three-years-old at the time), shoved my hand-written, stapled -together first edition of my book, *ABC's of Success…*, into my lap and said, "Read it," his words encouraged me.

I had written this book for Zachary before he was born, and as I told him later, "I wrote this for you while you were still in my belly." I knew he could learn how to do just about anything from reading.

At times, prior to yOur BackYard publishing and releasing *ABC's of Success...*, I had felt like giving up on my dream to become a published author. One crisp fall day at the Grand Ole Opry in Nashville, Tennessee, however, God used Tony Robbins, a motivational speaker and author, to strengthen my faltering resolve.

Tony's encouraging attitude and words throughout my day working as his personal assistant inspired me to continue with my writing career. Tony said, "If you talk about it, it's a dream. If you envision it, it's possible. If you schedule it, it's real." From these and other of Tony's encouraging words, I knew I had to not only envision and schedule steps to become a published author, but I also had to take that first step and start working with a professional editor and publisher.

In addition to encouraging myself, today, I encourage Taylor and other aspiring writers to "Just take that first step..." I also urge other "artists" to, "Read it...," to learn as much as possible about what it takes to make your dream a reality... to never ever never give up on your dreams.

"Just take that first step..." Even if, especially if you're tempted to cave into the tempting thought, "Why? What's the use?"

Solomon, a wise king who lived thousands of years ago, said, there's "nothing new under the sun." Nevertheless, remember, only you can do that something you do, the unique way you do it, even writing a cookbook...

Step by step by step...

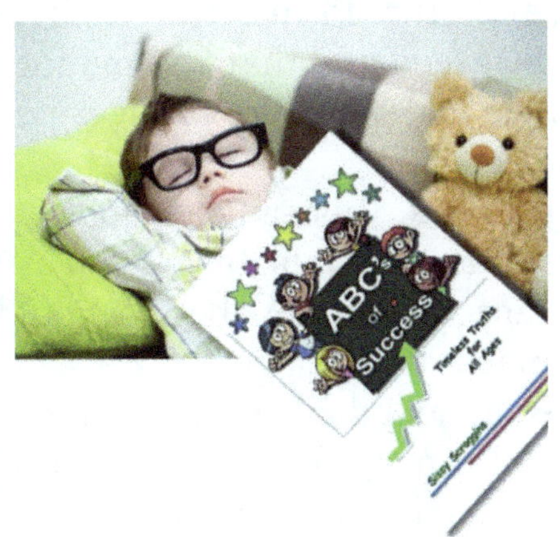

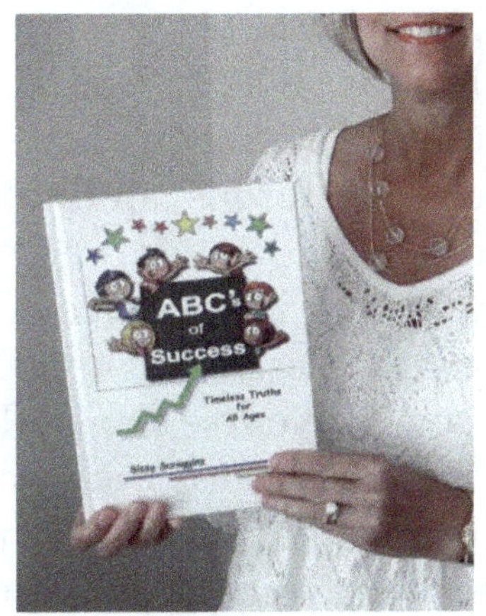

A Healthy Change

by

Anthony Terry

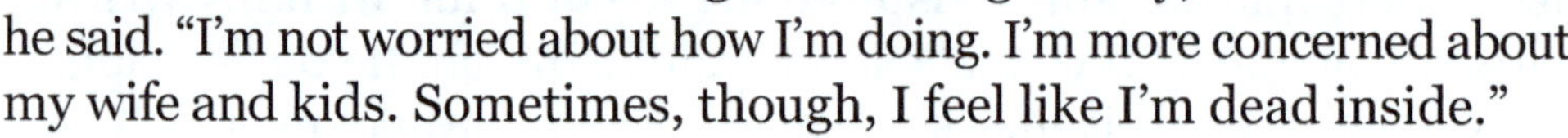

"Sometimes, I feel like I'm dead inside."

Recently, when talking with Mark, a married friend with two children, I asked him, "How are you doing? Are you happy?"

Mark stared back at me with a "deer in the headlights" look. "Well... Well, I'm working and making money," he said. "I'm not worried about how I'm doing. I'm more concerned about my wife and kids. Sometimes, though, I feel like I'm dead inside."

I nodded. "Whenever you get into your career and you settle, you usually work your scheduled 9 to 5; or sometimes a 7 to 3 shift, but then you may become complacent. At that point, you need to do something different. Maybe you should schedule a regular time together with your wife and kids in the gym. That way, you will be able to spend time with them as a family, and at the same time invest in your health. Working out on a regular basis not only improves your mental and physical health, but it can help you financially as well. By financially, I mean that you are not spending money as much on trivial things. You are investing time in your body to make it better, to get healthier.

"Instead of work..., work..., work..., which in a sense can become like a prison, you need to clear your path to be free," I told Mark. "You need to take time to make time for yourself... to take care of yourself... to exercise. It's OK to do that."

In my past, I did not value exercising. I did not enjoy power lifting like I do today. Instead of a way to de-stress, weightlifting seemed like a job. Now I realize that power lifting and other forms of exercising should be seen as a treat. Later, Mark agreed and thanked me for encouraging him to evaluate his lifestyle and make the changes he needed to do for his family and for himself.

Today, I encourage others as I urged Mark, "Instead of primarily focusing on trying to make money, examine and evaluate yourself as well as your lifestyle. Figure out what changes could work best for you. Set a goal for yourself to work out regularly.

If it helps, write down what you need to do. I don't write down my goals, but I visualize them in my mind. Writing goals down on paper, however, or typing them into a computer, helps some people.

Choose to be healthy. To get to the place you want to be, you have to work through diversions. Instead of exercising sporadically, make working out a regular part of your lifestyle. As Gabrielle Christina Victoria Douglas (Gabby Douglas), the first African American to become the Olympic individual all-around champion encouraged others:

Never quit, never give up.
When you have a little trouble here and there,
just keep fighting.
In the end, it will pay off.

Sometimes, when you're fighting to keep on keeping on, your work or something you're doing may weigh so heavy on you that you need to quit doing it. If you cannot quit, at least take a break. Choose to do something different.

Sometimes, like Mark, you may find yourself stressed out, depressed, or feel like you are drowning, simply because you do not take time out for yourself. Also, like Mark, you may sometimes think, *I feel like I'm dead inside.* That's the time to choose to do something different.

When making choices, consider your feelings, remembering feelings change and that what you choose can change you *and* your feelings. Also, remember that to take care of yourself, you have to take time for you. You have to take time to not only exercise, you have to give your mind and body time to rest.

No one else can make the choice to take better care of yourself than you. If you do not take care of yourself, who will? When making choices relating to change, remember what matters most in your life. When you do what you need to do to get to that place you truly want to be, a real joy will overtake you.

Today, if you need to change, choose to do something different. Instead of feeling dead inside—you will begin to live.

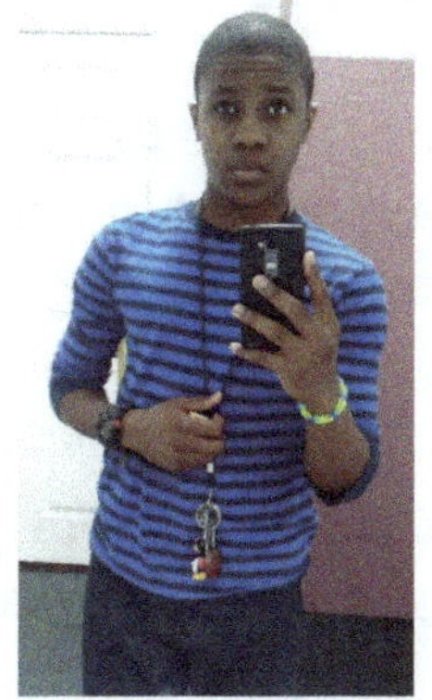 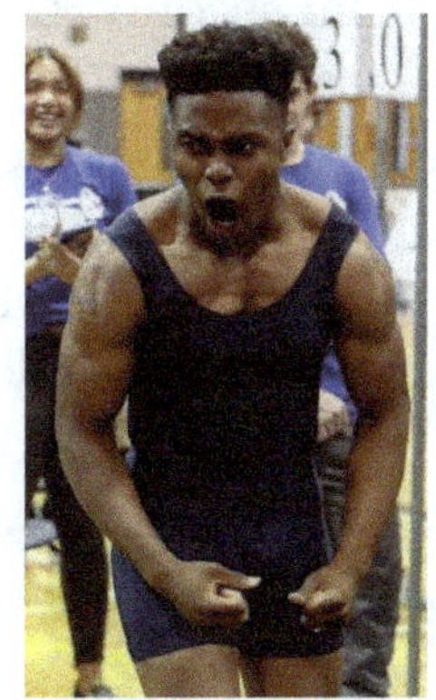

No Excuse

Bill McDonald

If I only had the time, I thought, during a busy season of my life, I *would go turkey hunting.*

My unscheduled 45-minute hunt started early one morning as I was returning from Nashville to Centerville, Tennessee, feeling "just plain tired;" like Old Man Sleep was tugging at my eyelids. Up to this point in turkey season, I had not killed a turkey.

From the distance that day, I watched the young Tom strutting his stuff on the almost four-acre "food plat" next to the oak tree line on the right-hand side of the field. Tom was doing his best to impress the three hens feeding... like I wasn't even there. I watched as he danced in the narrow tractor road to the place where the woods opened just enough to tolerate the once used logging road entrance, down the side of the overhanging limbs.

With his head the color of a new red-Vette, and his tail in full spread, Tom followed the trio of ladies into the shade. He gobbled just as he turned to enter the woods as if to warn any competitors considering they might have a chance with his gals....

That night, Tom browned up just right in the skillet. Along with the fresh morel mushrooms and the mashed potatoes and gravy, he made a feast fit for a king. Looking back at my unplanned turkey hunt, I am reminded once more of the importance of taking advantage of any opportunity that comes our way, and of the value of using time wisely.

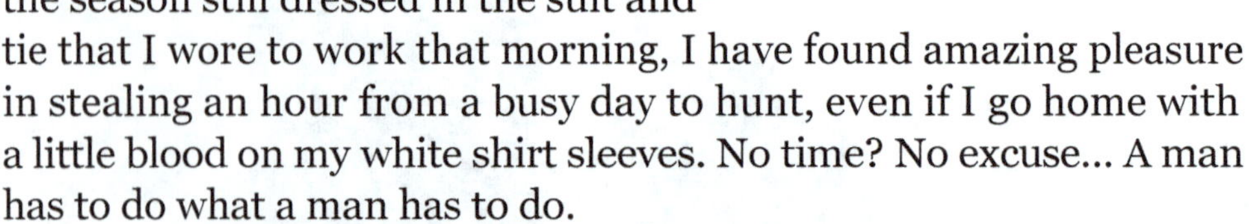

Now, as on that second Saturday of the season still dressed in the suit and tie that I wore to work that morning, I have found amazing pleasure in stealing an hour from a busy day to hunt, even if I go home with a little blood on my white shirt sleeves. No time? No excuse... A man has to do what a man has to do.

**See then that ye walk circumspectly, ... wise,
Redeeming the time, because the days are evil.**
~ Ephesians 5:15-16

Whatever You do—Do Your Best
by
Lahcen Belkimite

"Do you understand me?"

"Do you understand what I mean?"

"Do you speak English?"

"No," I sometimes had to answer during that fall of 2006 when I first came to America. At that time, I not only struggled to understand what some people said to me, but also how to answer them the right way in my broken English.

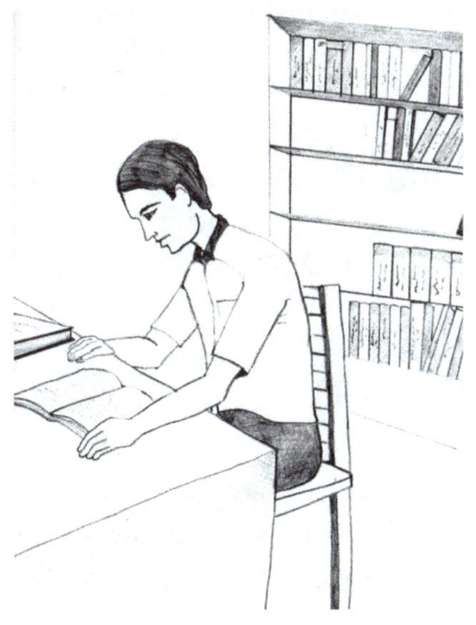

As I studied and struggled to learn to speak better English, if I did not understand what someone said to me, I would hand them my small notebook and pen and ask: "Will you write that down for me, please?"

When someone speaking to me asked, "Are you an American?" I proudly replied, "Yes."

Sometimes I might add, "Even though I was not born in America, but in Morocco, I am an American citizen."

I often thought, especially when someone noticed my foreign accent and appeared impatient with my imperfect English, *I may not yet understand some things about my new country, but I am learning more every day. As I learn, I am not only trying to do things right; I try to do the right things.*

I learned that to succeed, you have to listen. If you do not understand something, do not be ashamed to ask for help. If you do not understand what someone is saying, never criticize or make fun of them. They, like me when I first started learning English, need someone to listen to try to help them learn as much as they can.

I understand what it's like to feel frustrated when you can't understand what someone talking to you means. I not only speak English; I speak the human language—the language of kindness... the language of love for others as we love ourselves. That's not only one of the right things to do, that's the only right thing to do—no matter our country. I understand that...

Struggling to Give God Control
by
Erin Murphy Anderson

Prior to 1988, traveling by air did not bother me as much as it does now. Now, I hate to fly. When I know I plan to fly somewhere, I become anxious. Sometimes, because I know I will not have any control of the airplane, I not only worry about what might happen, I become visibly upset. *What if?* thoughts often attack my mind.

What if the plane malfunctions and crashes? What if a terrorist hijacks the plane? What if someone has planted a bomb on the plane and it explodes and kills all the passengers?

While attending college in Greensburg, Pennsylvania, at the age of 20, I, along with three other female college students, Kate, Beth, and Elyse, flew to London to attend college for the August to December semester. At the end of time, we discussed the idea of staying an extra week to travel and see more of the sites.

It'll be fun, I thought. After all, we had studied hard and who knew when we might have the opportunity to travel overseas again. Kate, however, hesitated. "I'm sorry," she said, "I cannot afford to stay any longer. I have to go home. You all can stay and have fun. I will see you back in the States."

"No," I insisted. "My finances are a bit tight as well. I will go home with you."

On December 14, 1988, Kate and I said goodbye to Beth and Elyse. We boarded our British Airways flight with the promise, "We will see you when you get home."

Beth and Elyse never made it back to America. They both died when a bomb exploded on their plane.

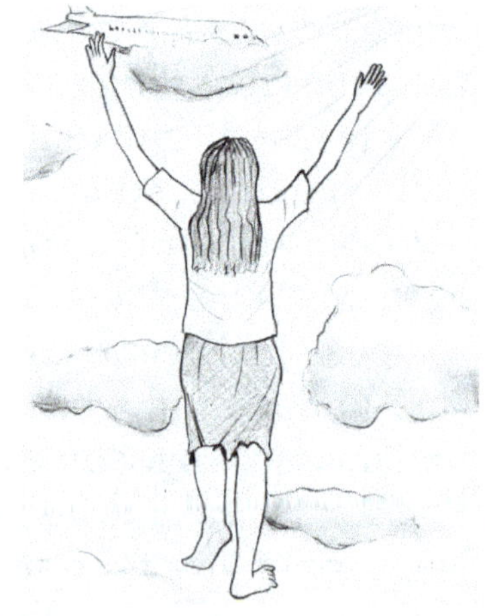

God left me here for a reason, I often thought. While I may not understand God's plan, I know that part of the reason is to encourage others that in life and even when it comes to death—God, not you nor I, remains in control. Meantime, as we walk beside each other in this life we are to be there for and help each other "on the way home."

Choose to Love
John Vennell, PhD.

"I hate you...."

Although I never heard Aunt Phyllis specifically tell someone, "I hate you," the way she treated our family members, her clients, and others taught me "how to hate." Before becoming a "boss" as a renowned veterinarian, Aunt Phyllis, my maternal aunt, worked as a horse trainer.

Aunt Phyllis made it plain that she thought she was better than others. In a store, instead of waiting in line to buy something, if she were not at the front of the line, she would leave.

"Waiting in line is for commoners," she told me. "I don't wait."

Aunt Phyllis refused to offer a minute of grace to others. She could be late, I noticed—but others had better be on time. As she inadvertently taught me to how to hate, God taught me how to pray for and love those who, like Aunt Phyllis, appeared to be unloving.

The year after my dad died when I was 12, God, in His grace and love, saved me. When a 15-year-old student at our Christian school shared the gospel with me, I received the good news and believed in Jesus. I knew that I had been "born again."

Evenings after I worked for Aunt Phyllis on her farm, she made me read to her from medical books. One day, instead of reading as usual, I opened my Bible and read John 15 to Aunt Phyllis. In this chapter, Jesus explains that He is "the true vine..."; that some branches bear fruit while others do not; that "the branch cannot bear fruit of itself, except it abide in the vine; no more can ye, except ye abide in me."

"What does that mean?" Aunt Phyllis asked me.

At 13, although I did my best, I did not do a good job of answering that and other questions. In time, as God changed me and called me to preach the gospel, I studied, learned, and memorized Scriptures. I learned that God and His love were bigger than me and my limitations, bigger than Aunt Phyllis; even bigger than hate.

Sometimes, it's hard to love someone like Aunt Phyllis. In Jesus Christ, I have learned that love not only never fails—it conquers hate.

Instead of telling someone, "I hate you," I encourage others to pray for those who appear unloving... to love them. When we follow Jesus, He teaches us to choose to love... even those like Aunt Phyllis.

Owe no man any thing, but to love one another...
~ Romans 13:8

From Fear to Faith

shELAH*

God's out to get me…

Years ago, while sitting on Death Row in Riverbend Maximum Security Institute, with six men convicted of murder, I smiled. I suddenly realized, *I'm not afraid.*

With that revelation, inside that small concrete-walled classroom, I breathed a prayer of thanks.

Dear Heavenly Father, I'm not sure how You did that for me, but Thank You. Thank You: for changing me from someone terrified to look someone else in the eyes; from someone full of fear, thinking that for every time I sinned, You were "out to get me" and send me to Hell. Thank You for saving me…for taking away my fear; for making me Your child; for giving Your Son, Jesus Christ, to die on the cross to become the only Way to "get me" and others to Heaven.

Before my legally blind, Pentecostal mother came to the place in her life where she realized that God did not send Jesus into the world to condemn us (John 3:17), she would sometimes warn me:

> ➢ If you wear lipstick, you're going to Hell.
> ➢ If you wear shorts, you're going to Hell,
> ➢ If you go to a movie, you're going to Hell.

Instead of heeding Mother's warnings I often sneaked away from home and painted my lips like Ruby in Kenny Roger's song. Sometimes, at my only friend's house, [I only had one] I changed from my dress into shorts, and once before I got a part-time job at a theatre, I watched a movie.

The fear of what might happen next, however, relentlessly tormented me. Years and years and years before Mother divorced my alcoholic father, the bad things I feared, happened over and over and over. Inside the temporary places we called "home," the devil in the bottle regularly turned my dad into a violent man police often escorted to jail.

Outside home, more often than not, when someone spoke to me, I lowered my eyes, unable to communicate.

At the age of 9, I sometimes sporadically attended church. One Sunday night, I remember that when the preacher talked about what the Roman soldiers did before they crucified Jesus, I could not hold back my tears. Pilate had ordered the soldiers to flog Jesus. When scourging or flogging people, soldiers used a whip with bits of lead and stone entwined into it. Soldiers whipped Jesus' back to shreds, yet

He prayed, "Father, forgive them..." As I listened, I tried to wipe the tears that kept flooding my face.

"Jesus willingly suffered that horrific death on the cross for you and me," the preacher said, "so that we may have eternal life. Jesus loves you and willingly gave His life to pay the penalty for your sins. If you will trust Him, He will save you."

I remember that night in church as I knelt and prayed, "Jesus, save me," I did not even try to stop my tears.

Later after Mother and Dad divorced, God used Mother to force me at the age of 11, and my three younger siblings. to walk several miles to church not only on Sunday mornings, but also on Sunday nights. When we met in groups, teachers in church would challenge us to memorize Bible verses. We even had to attend Wednesday night services and listen to that preacher read and preach from the Bible.

But then, we stopped going to church.

I did not start attending church regularly again until years later after Jim and I married. Like my mother had done to me, I forced our four children to go to church. Sunday mornings; Sunday nights; Wednesday Nights; Revivals; Youth groups; Summer Camps. In time, Randall, Dawn, Daniel and Donna asked Jesus to save them. He did.

Jesus also continued to work in me to increase my faith and hope as Philippians 1:6 promises, "Being confident of this very thing, that he which hath begun a good work in you will perform it until the day of Jesus Christ..."

While teaching a writing class that day years ago on Death Row, I not only realized, *I'm not afraid*, I got to share the reminder, "Jesus loves you. He will save you...." In my day-to-day life outside of Death Row, I get to do as the Bible directs in 1 Peter 3:15, to "be ready always to give an answer to every man that asketh you a reason of the hope that is in you."

Writing out experiences in my life to share hope in Jesus gives me opportunities to communicate the good news to some who may not yet know Jesus; that He loves them.

Today, I "get to" tell others that when I used to think, *God's out to get me...*, it turned out to be true. He's also out to get you—for good in His grace and love; to free you from fear; to give you eternal life here on Earth as well as in Heaven....

* To share the reason for the "hope that is in you," email:
yourbackyard@gmail.com

When Lightning Flashes
Logan Winstead

I love lightning.

Lightning can heat air surrounding it up to five times hotter than the temperature of the sun's surface. As the lightning's heat causes the air surrounding it to rapidly expand and vibrate, it produces the rolling thunder we hear shortly after we see a flash of lightning.

Watching the bright flashes of light; hearing the thundering roar that follows totally relaxes me. Concentrating on the intense power controlling the lightning brings a sense of peace to my sometimes-troubled mind.

At the age of 9, Rebecca, my stepsister and I (10 at that time) were watching a thunderstorm from the large window in my dad's bedroom. Suddenly, a bolt of lightning struck the huge oak tree 20 feet from our house. We screamed. As the thunder roared and rattled our house, Rebecca, and I ran out of Dad's bedroom. Later, I went back and continued to watch the lightning flash.

As a young father, I learned that even though we go through storms in life, God remains in control. When Sarah, my seven-month-old daughter died seven years ago, Heather, her mother, and I felt like our hearts had been struck by lightning. My anger (hurt turned outward) because of Sarah's death, consumed me. I struck out at God.

Over time, as I kept searching for answers, God gave me a sense of peace. Sarah's death helped me realize that when it's your time to die, it's your time. As God gave me "the peace that surpasses understanding," my anger dissipated.

Now, I encourage others that instead of letting worry and anger consume them during their storms in life, they can find comfort and peace by relinquishing whatever happens into God's hands. He controls lightning. He has the last Word regarding life and death.

Today, I still love lightning. Lightning makes me think of our Heavenly Father. He taught me that no matter the storm... no matter how fiercely it threatens, He remains in control.

**Canst thou send lightnings,
that they may go and say unto thee, Here we are?**
~ Job 38:35

Why I Changed My Name to Hope

I still remember how hopeless we (families of the three NGO imprisoned human rights activists) felt when we traveled to Changsha 19 times seeking information about our loved ones, the ChangSha3, but never received any information. We only knew that Chinese Communist Party (CCP) authorities had dismissed their lawyers and assigned CCP lawyers to convince them to plead guilty.

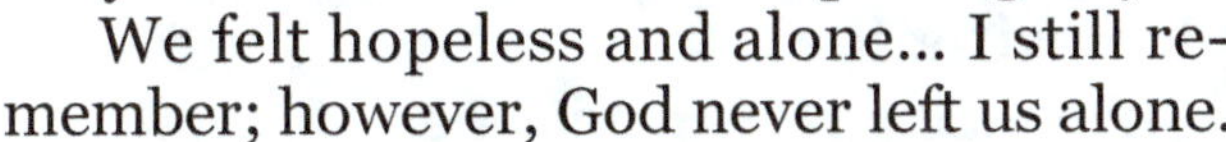
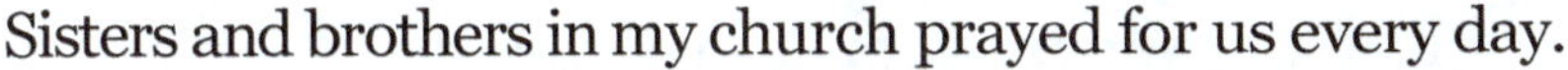
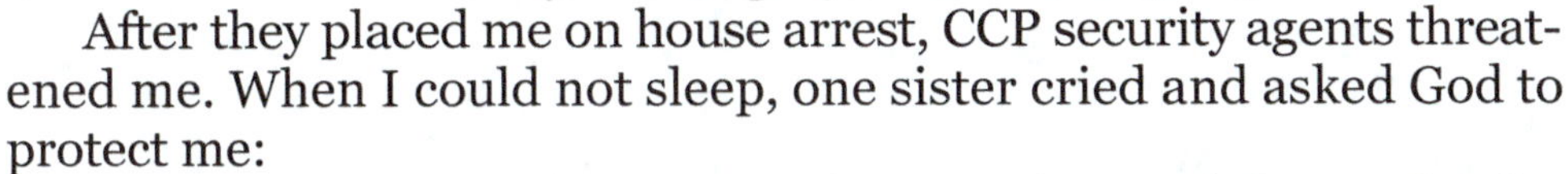

We felt hopeless and alone... I still remember; however, God never left us alone. Sisters and brothers in my church prayed for us every day.

After they placed me on house arrest, CCP security agents threatened me. When I could not sleep, one sister cried and asked God to protect me:

> My Father, I ask you to protect Sister Shi... Hide her under the shadow of thy wings. She is your daughter, ...no one can rule over her... Please give your peace and hope to her.

Because of security concerns, I did not tell anyone when I left China. When they did not hear from me as usual, five brothers and sisters went to my house to try to find me that night. When I arrived in the United States (US) and heard this, I cried. I knew they were showing God's love.

One day, I felt so sick... I felt I could not go any further. That day, I prayed like Jesus prayed in Gethsemane, "Father, ...take this cup from me. But not my will... Your will be done."

Jesus spoke to my heart, "I know. I know everything about you."

When I arrived in Midland, Texas, Pastor Fu, and *ChinaAid* staff, with Christian brothers and sisters, warmly welcomed us. They had prepared a place for my daughter and me to stay, brought food, toys, books, and necessary items for us, more than we needed. God answered our prayers...

That's why, in the United States, I changed my name to Hope.

**Hope deferred makes the heart sick,
but a longing fulfilled is a tree of life.**
~Proverbs 13:12

Hang on to Hope

"I get up every time I fall down," Paul Harvey Aurandt (1918-2009), popularly known as Paul Harvey, a long-time radio broadcaster for ABC, said.

In the book, *More than Enough*, Dave Ramsey shares about a time he lost hope. "…In the middle of our financial disaster, I was reading my Bible as the sun came up and discovered this Scripture, Romans 5:3-4:"

**And not only that,
but we also glory in tribulations,
knowing that
tribulation produces perseverance,
and perseverance, character,
and character hope.**

When we go through troubles, we learn to "hang on." Hanging on to hope during tough times changes us for the better.

- Hope, an act of will, is a decision.
- Don't let failure steal your hope.
- With hope, instead of being stuck, you act.

Optimism is the faith that leads to achievement.
Nothing can be done without hope and confidence.
~ Helen Keller

Darkness comes. In the middle of it, the future looks blank. The temptation to quit is huge. Don't.
You are in good company…
You will argue with yourself that there is no way forward.
But with God, nothing is impossible.
He has more ropes and ladders and tunnels out of pits than you can conceive.
Wait.
Pray without ceasing.
Hope.
~ John Piper

Hands

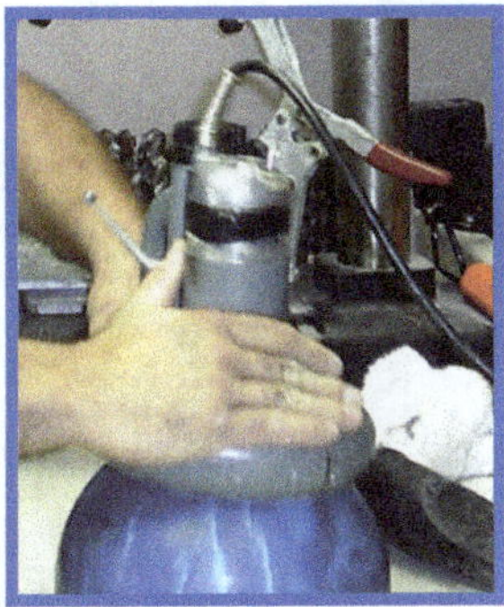

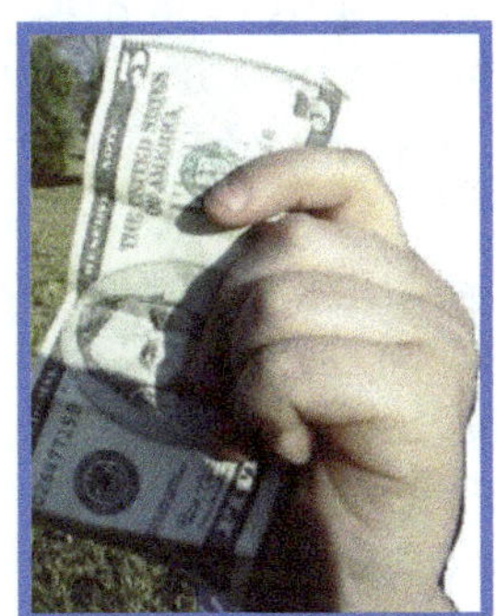

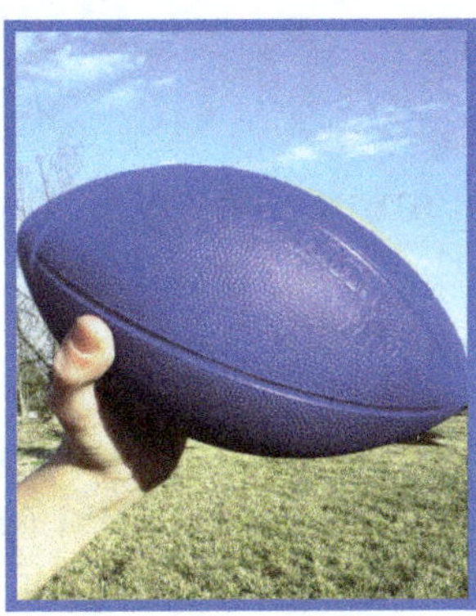

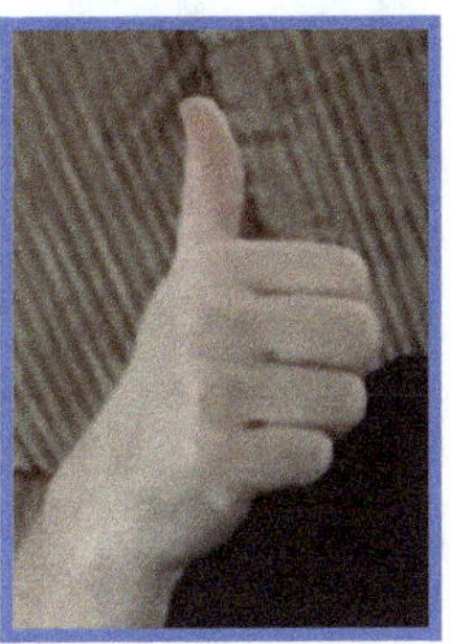

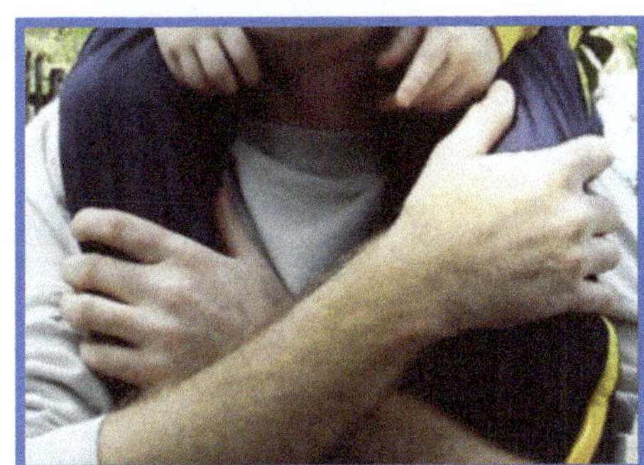

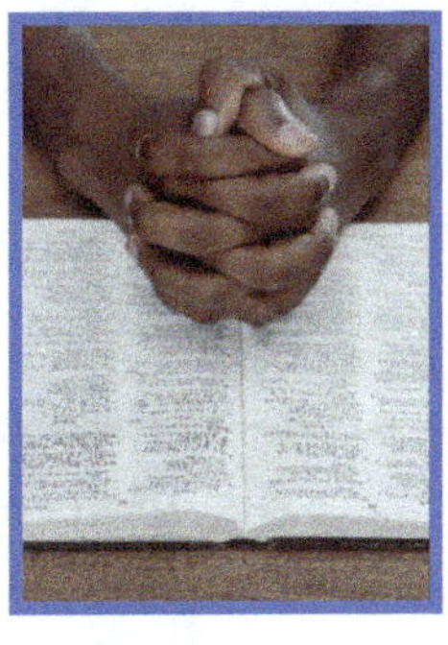

Designed
by
shELAH

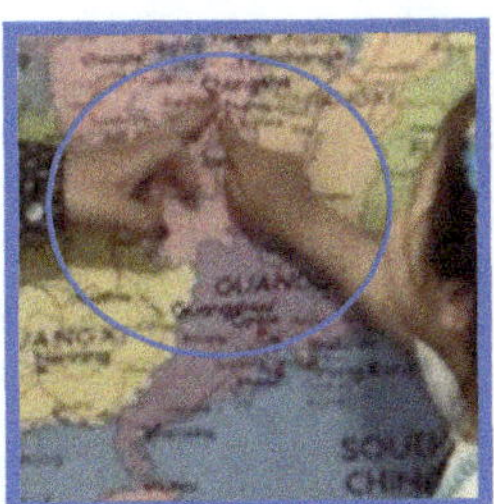

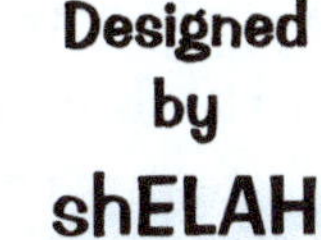

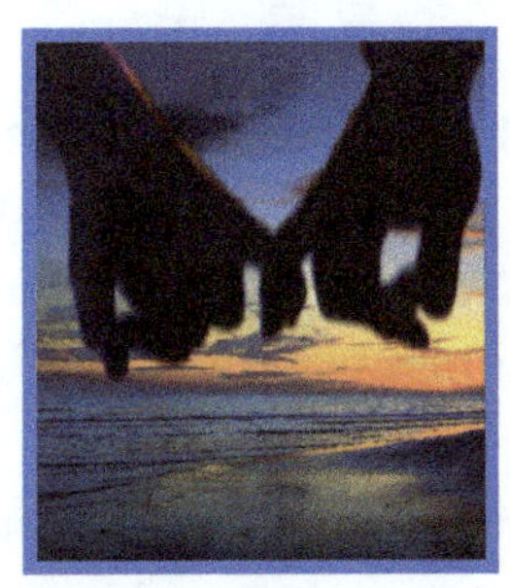

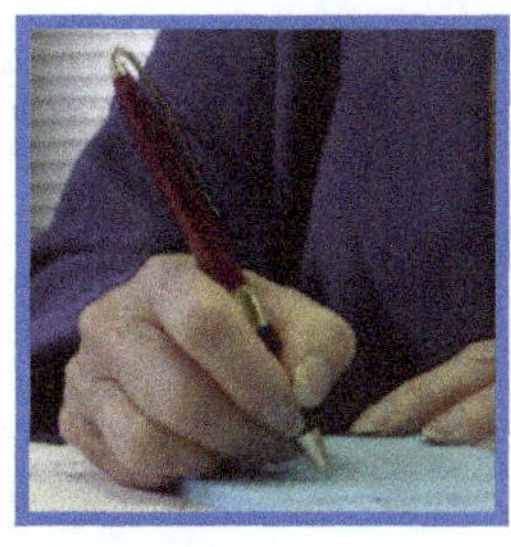

**Whatsoever thy hand findeth to do,
do it with thy might;...**

~ Ecclesiastes 9:10

Music—Then
Frances (Fanny) Jane Crosby
(1820-1915)

Fanny Crosby, an American poetess and one of the most prolific hymnists in history, composed more than 8,000 hymns. Fanny's hymns include:

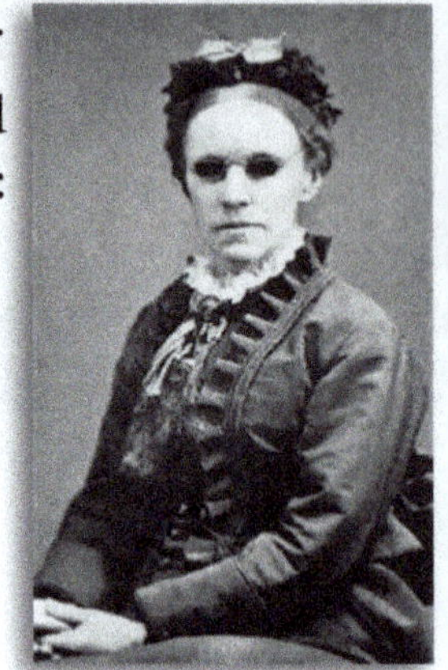

> - Rescue the Perishing
> - Blessed Assurance
> - All the Way My Savior Leads Me
> - Pass Me Not My Gentle Savior
> - Near the Cross
> - To God Be the Glory
> - I am Thine, O Lord
> - He Hideth My Soul
> - Saved by Grace

Fanny published her first book of poems, *The Blind Girl and Other Poems*, in 1844. At one point in her life, she sold her poems for $2.00 each and used the money to help support her work with the poor.

Today, many continue to sing "To God be the Glory."

To God be the glory, great things He hath done,
So loved He the world that He gave us His Son,
Who yielded His life our redemption to win,
And opened the life-gate that all may go in.

Praise the Lord, praise the Lord,
Let the earth hear His voice;
Praise the Lord, praise the Lord,
Let the people rejoice;
Oh, come to the Father, through Jesus the Son,
And give Him the glory; great things He hath done.

**O sing unto the Lord a new song:
sing unto the Lord, all the earth.**
~ Psalm 96:1

Music — Now
Born to Be Special
Jerry Arhelger

Men marvel at the value that they put on gold
But they can count the many treasures that their hands can hold.
And in all of their searching, they will never find the worth
That God places on one little baby's birth.

Though diamonds may sparkle like the stars in the skies,
They can never match the beauty found in a baby's eyes.
The face filled with wonder, the heart filled with love,
Even God's greatest gift was a Child from above.

Children are born to be special.
It's so obvious, even blinded eyes should see.
When a child is in the room, they can lift the darkest gloom,
And they can reveal the joy of eternity.
Children are born to be special

But they need our help until they're fully grown.
That what treasures they do make, when in love we take
Those born to be special into a special home.
Look all around you from without and from within.
See if you can find something greater than them.
The little hands that reach out and touch our hearts so tight.

Who would ever want to not allow their light—
To shine into the darkness around us everyday
And lead us in the path that little children see?
If all of us could be just children once again,
I'm sure we would remember how special they are then.

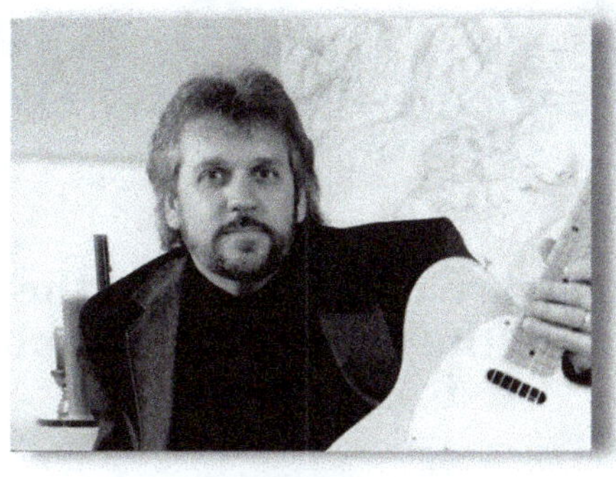

Born to Be Special

Jerry Arhelger

The one thing all of us have in common is not the ability to give birth but the bond of being born.

Each one of us shares the common bond of the birth canal... moving from the nurtured comfort of the womb to bright lights and cold calculating hands. Our trauma of this birthing experience was only lessened by the bosom or loving caress of someone who expressed his or her belief that we were born to be special.

If we were blessed in being held at just the right moment, encouraged with the possibility that we can achieve our dreams, we have a good chance that we will leave a special mark on those that we encounter in our lives. But if we were discarded, left to believe that we are no more than a mistake, we normally will produce more mistakes in a desperate hope to have someone recognize that we do exist and have purpose.

If we have been ignored or abused, we might be blessed with someone or circumstances that reveal our special stealth to show stuff to us. I have met many who have conquered their future by the comfort of escaping that their birth was not a chance encounter, a passion, or loss, but that it was a carefully designed plan of God.

God never intended in His divine plan that any birth would be looked upon as less than special.

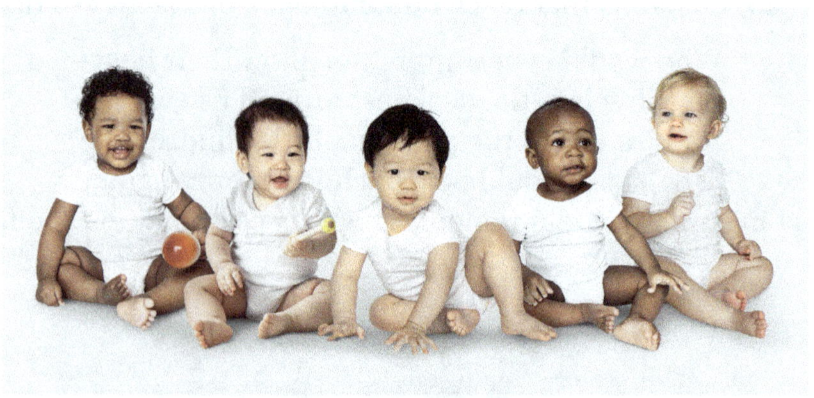

**Lo,
children are an heritage of the Lord:
and the fruit of the womb
is his reward.**
~Psalm 127:3

This Too Shall Pass

Sometimes I laugh. Sometimes I cry
And I can't help but wonder why
Some things will happen in our lives
But that's OK. This too shall pass.
God knows the things we all will face.
And He will help us in our race.
He'll be with us forevermore
No matter what we have in store.

I'll pray for you. Please pray for me
When times are hard and we can't see
The way that we must surely go.
He'll show the way when we don't know.
He knows our needs. He'll hold my hand
Until before his throne I'll stand.
The truth to me is clear as glass.
His promise is "This too shall pass."

~ Excerpt from Poem by LouEllen Hoffman

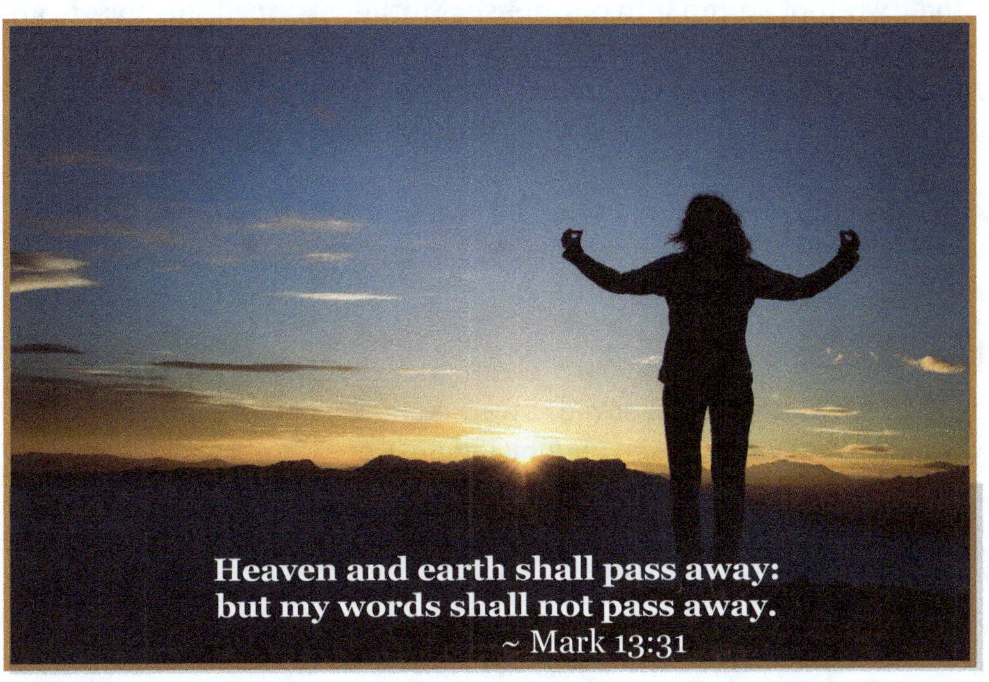

3-D Reflections
Opie

"Stop it!"

At times, while growing up in the country, I wanted to scream out at several girls in school who taunted and bullied me, "Stop it!" But then, I remembered my sweet Mama's words, "Opie, you know we don't live like other people. We live with what we have…. We don't worry about what we don't have."

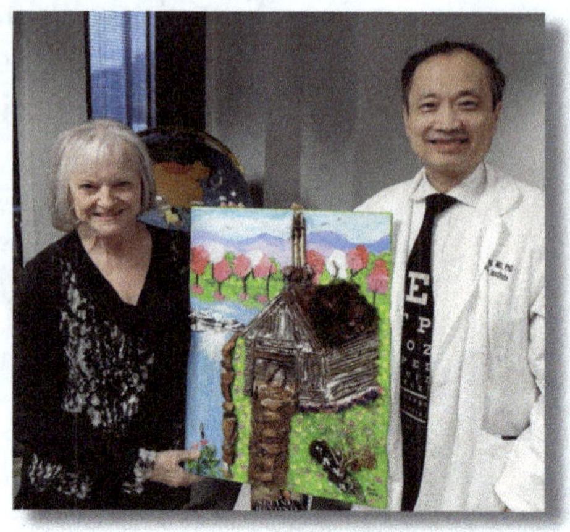

Mother taught me that you can take almost nothing and make something. Whenever cooking a meal, if Mother did not have all the ingredients a recipe called for, she simply left that something out and didn't worry about it. One day at the age of 10, I heard Mother say that she needed a table for her lamp. With five children to feed and only $25 a week for groceries, buying anything other than necessities was impossible. Instead of complaining, Mother walked out into the woods behind our house and found a stump from an oak tree that had been cut down. After she dragged that two-foot stump into our house, Mother stripped the bark from the sides. She then opened a can of Johnson Floor Wax we had and grabbed a gigantic glob with her hands. Then starting at the bottom of the stump, she then used the palms of her hands to coat her table.

Amazing, I thought.

Not long afterward, I began creating my unique three-dimensional (3-D) paintings. Each time I paint, I experience total joy…, not only during the process of painting but also when I get to share my work with others.

Growing up as a poor preacher's kid, I remember that for years, I secretly wanted to get saved. I wanted to "be born again," and have the new life Daddy talked about. God answered my heart's desire, my secret prayer, that year in camp.

Today, 64 years later, I can thankfully say, that because my Jesus is my everything, I have been walking with Him since that day, I said, "Yes! Yes! Yes!"

I never plan to "Stop it…."

The following photos reflect a sampling of the life and depth Opie's nature-enhanced creations reflect. "In real life," her extraordinary, unique paintings appear three-dimensional. In addition to painting and ministering from where she lives in the country, Opie's life stories encourage readers to appreciate the "works of art" our Heavenly Father creates in our lives.

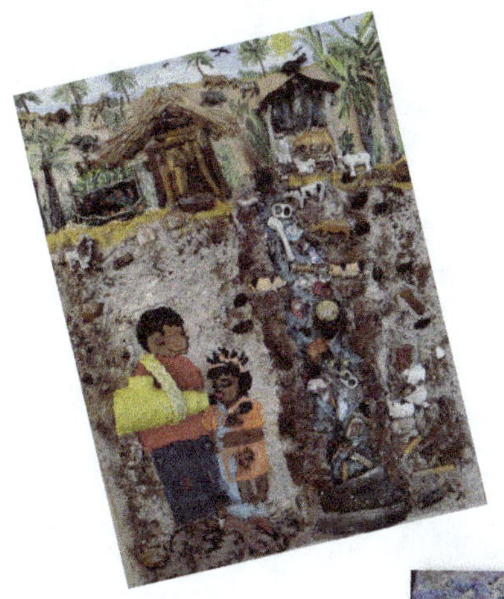

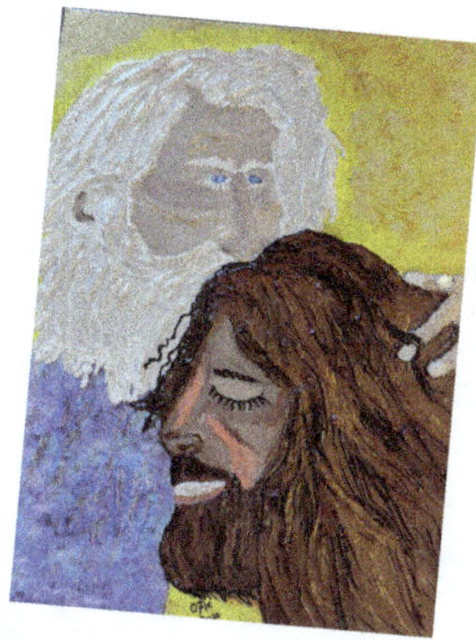

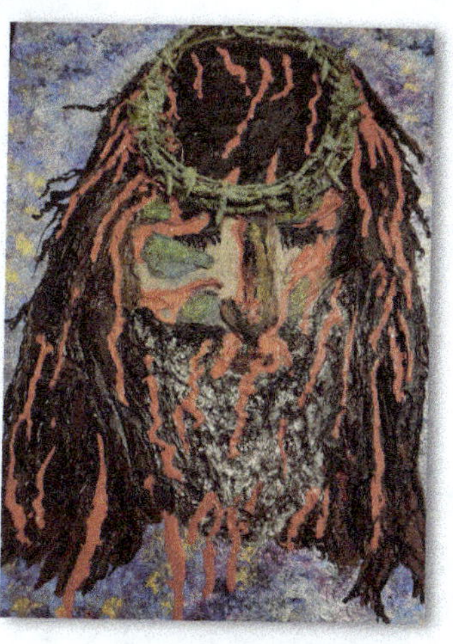

3-D Paintings
by
Opie

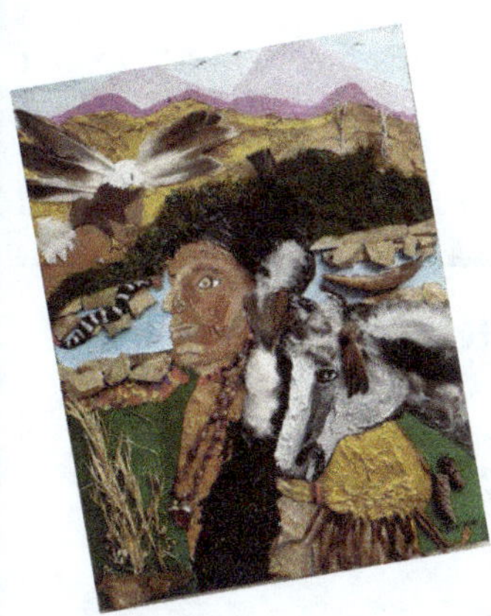

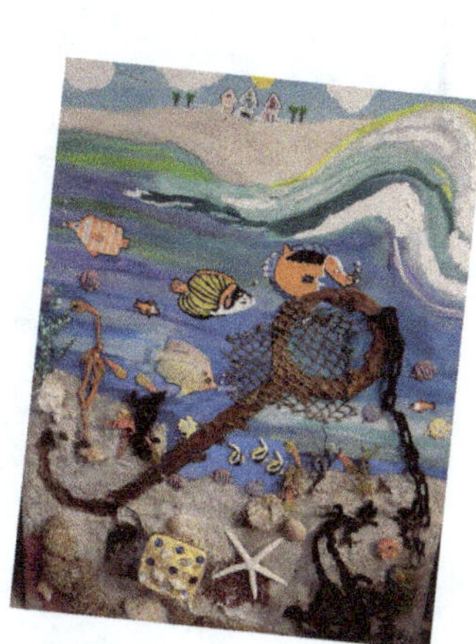

Art for All Ages

Draw picture of something you are thankful for...

O give thanks to the LORD
for he is good:
for his mercy endureth for ever.
~ Psalm 107:1

7 Things our Heavenly Father "Knoweth"
that we need to remember—not to forget*

1. Our Heavenly Father knows our "secrets." Yet He loves us anyway. He knows our heart's desires, as well as what we pray. Jesus said: "But you, when you pray, go into your room, and when you have shut your door, pray to your Father who *is* in the secret *place;* and your Father who sees in secret will reward you openly." *Matthew 6:6*

2. Our Heavenly Father knows what we need—even if/when it's different than what we think we need. He promises to supply ALL our needs. Jesus said: "Therefore do not be like them (hypocrites). For your Father knows the things you have need of before you ask Him." *Matthew 6:8*

3. Our Heavenly Father knows if we harbor unforgiveness in our heart. He also knows how to help us forgive someone we think we can't. Jesus said: "For if you forgive men their trespasses, your heavenly Father will also forgive you." *Matthew 6:14*

4. Our Heavenly Father knows who/what we put first. Jesus said: "For where your treasure is, there your heart will be also." *Matthew 6:21*

5. Our Heavenly Father knows that each day, we get to choose life or death. Jesus said: "No one can serve two masters; for either he will hate the one and love the other, or else he will be loyal to the one and despise the other. You cannot serve God and mammon [money]" *Matthew 6:24*

6. Our Heavenly Father knows the answers to our worries. When we feel overwhelmed, He will help us through tough times. Jesus said: "Which of you by worrying can add one cubit to his stature?" *Matthew 6:27*

7. Our Heavenly Father knows about our tomorrows. He will never fail us. Jesus said: "Therefore do not worry about tomorrow, for tomorrow will worry about its own things. Sufficient for the day *is* its own trouble." *Matthew 6:34*

*Verses: NKJV

For your Father knows the things you have need of before you ask Him.

~ Matthew 6:8

Anonymously Yours
A. Nonymous

Psalm 23 in Cyberspace Language

The Lord is my programmer,
I shall not crash.
He installed His software on the hard disk of my heart,
All of His commands are user friendly,
His directory moves me to the right choices for His name's sake.
Even though I scroll through the problems of life,
I will fear no bugs, for You are my backup;
Your password protects me;
You prepare a menu before me in the presence of my enemies;
Your help is only a key away.
Surely goodness and mercy will follow me all the days of my life,
And my file will be merged with His and saved forever.

When God Sends People—
Sometimes, They Make Excuses

Abraham was too old. Moses stuttered. Miriam was a gossip.
Jacob was a liar. Gideon doubted. Elijah was burned out.
First David's armor didn't fit; then he had an affair,
and had someone killed. Solomon was too rich.
Isaiah had unclean lips. Jeremiah was too young.
Jonah didn't like the job.
Amos's only training was in the school of fig-tree pruning.
Naomi was a widow. Peter was afraid of death.
Thomas was from Missouri (the "show-me" state)
Paul was a murderer. Mark was rejected by Paul.
Timothy had ulcers. Lazarus was dead.
Martha was a worry-wart.
....or so they claimed, before God's Spirit
empowered them to rise to the occasion
and become some of the greatest heroes of our faith.

The Center of the Bible

What is the shortest chapter in the Bible?
Psalm 117

What is the longest chapter in the Bible?
Psalm 119

Which chapter is in the center of the Bible?
Psalm 118

There are 594 chapters before Psalm 118.

There are 594 chapters after Psalm 118.

Add these numbers up and you get 1188.

What is the center verse in the Bible?
Psalm 118:8

Does this verse say something significant
about God's perfect will for our lives?

The next time someone says
they would like to find
God's perfect will for their lives
and that they want to be
in the center of His Will,
just send them to
the center of His Word!
~ Author Unknown

**It is better to trust in the LORD
than to put confidence in man.**
~Psalm 118:8

Words from and about "The Word"

The Bible, the most up-to-date book in the world, never grows old. "Eternal, yet ever new, its messages of the ancient past are just as poignant and vital to the men of today...." More than 1500 years ago, during different times in history, 40 authors wrote the words we know as "the Word." Enemies have targeted and attacked the Holy Bible like no other book, yet it remains the best-selling book of all times. No archaeological discovery contradicts a biblical reference.

The Bible foretold the roundness of the Earth. Isaiah 40:22 states, "It is he [the Lord God] that sitteth upon **the circle of the earth**...." Psalm 147:4 recounts, "He telleth the number of the stars; he calleth them all by their names." Leviticus 17:11 states, "For the life of the flesh is in the blood." This "Word," from 3500 years ago tells us that blood serves as the source of life. Our medical world did not accept this scientific fact until after the end of the 18th century.

The book, *Can An Intelligent Person Believe The Bible?*,
By Louis T. Talbot, published 80 years ago in 1942 answers
a resounding "yes" to the following:

In this day of infidelity, rationalism, skepticism, modernism,
and other forms of unbelief,
can an intelligent person believe the Bible
to be the infallible, inerrant Word of God?

Yes...? Yes... Yes!

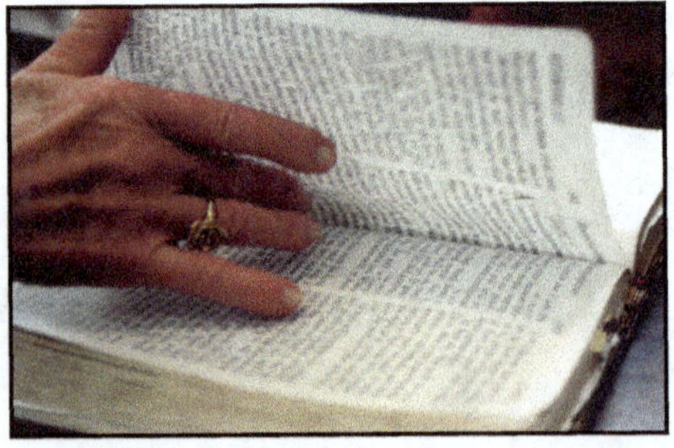

**Every Word of God is pure;
He is a shield
to those who put their trust in Him.**
~ Proverbs 30:5

Encouraging Faith

Years ago, a student attending the Mexican Indian Training Center in Veracruz, Mexico, drew this and several other biblical reflections.

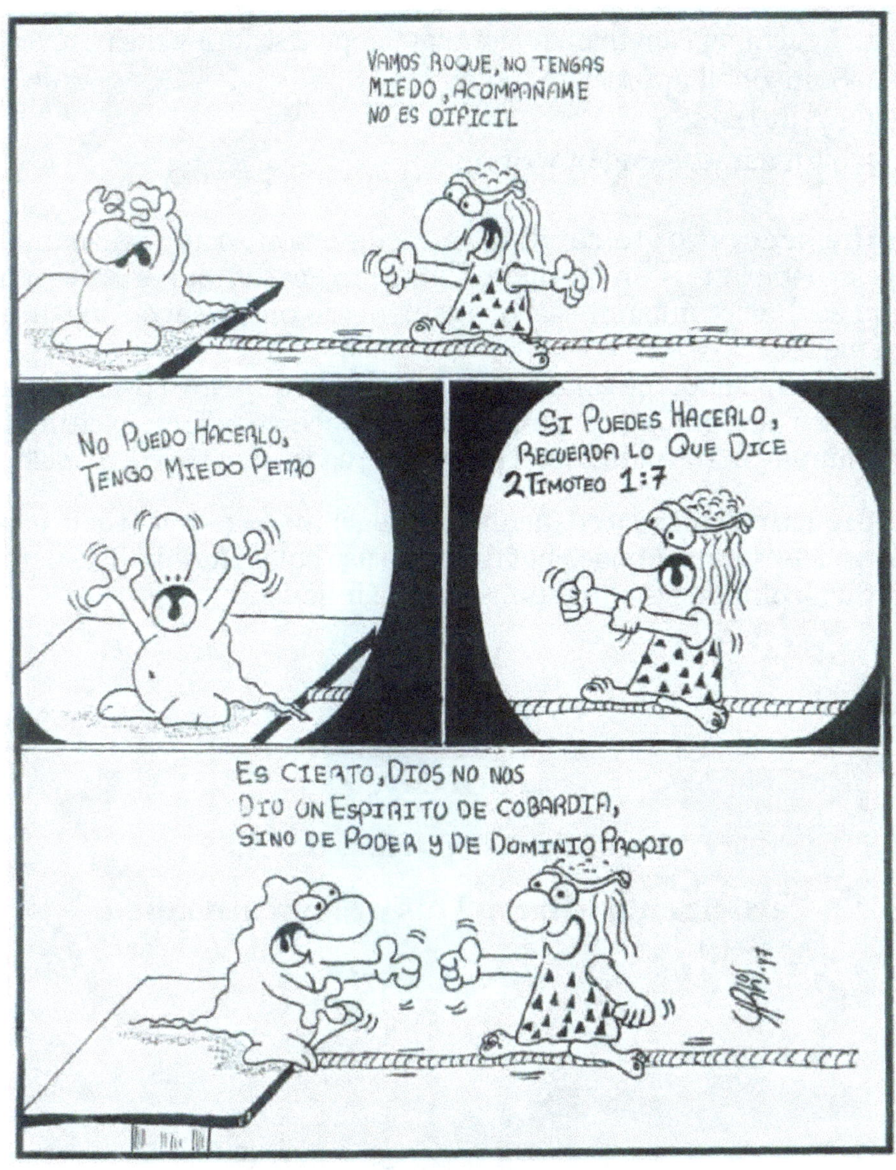

**For God has not given us a spirit of fear,
but of power and of love
and of a sound mind.**

~ 2 Timothy 1:7

Three Thanksgiving Notes

On one note card, have each person write out, draw, or have someone write for them:

1. Something I am thankful for that happened during the past year.
2. Someone I appreciate today.
3. I pray that...
4. Sign name at end of writing.

On the second note card, have each person write their name in large artistic letters on one side. Gather the cards and mix them up. Hand each person a note card, ensuring no one receives his or her own name.

The recipient of the card will then write out as many positive things about the person on the card he or she received. Time writing for three minutes. One person at a time then reads what they wrote aloud.

On the third note card, again have each person write their name in large letters on one side., but this time use bold lettering. The person will then complete their response to the following:

Today,

or

Each day,

if the Lord wills, I...

Participants will read his or her card aloud.

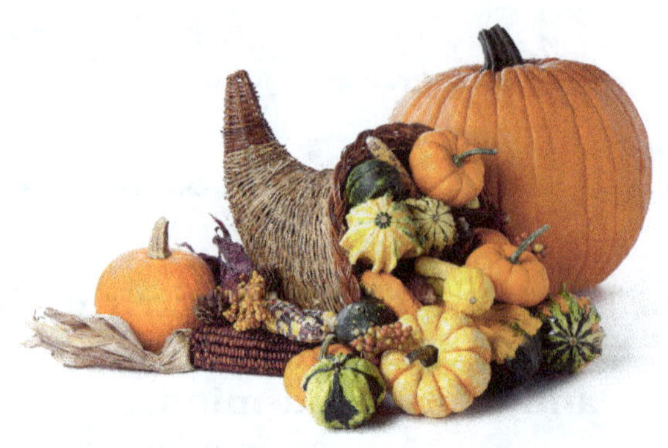

Health & Survival Stuff

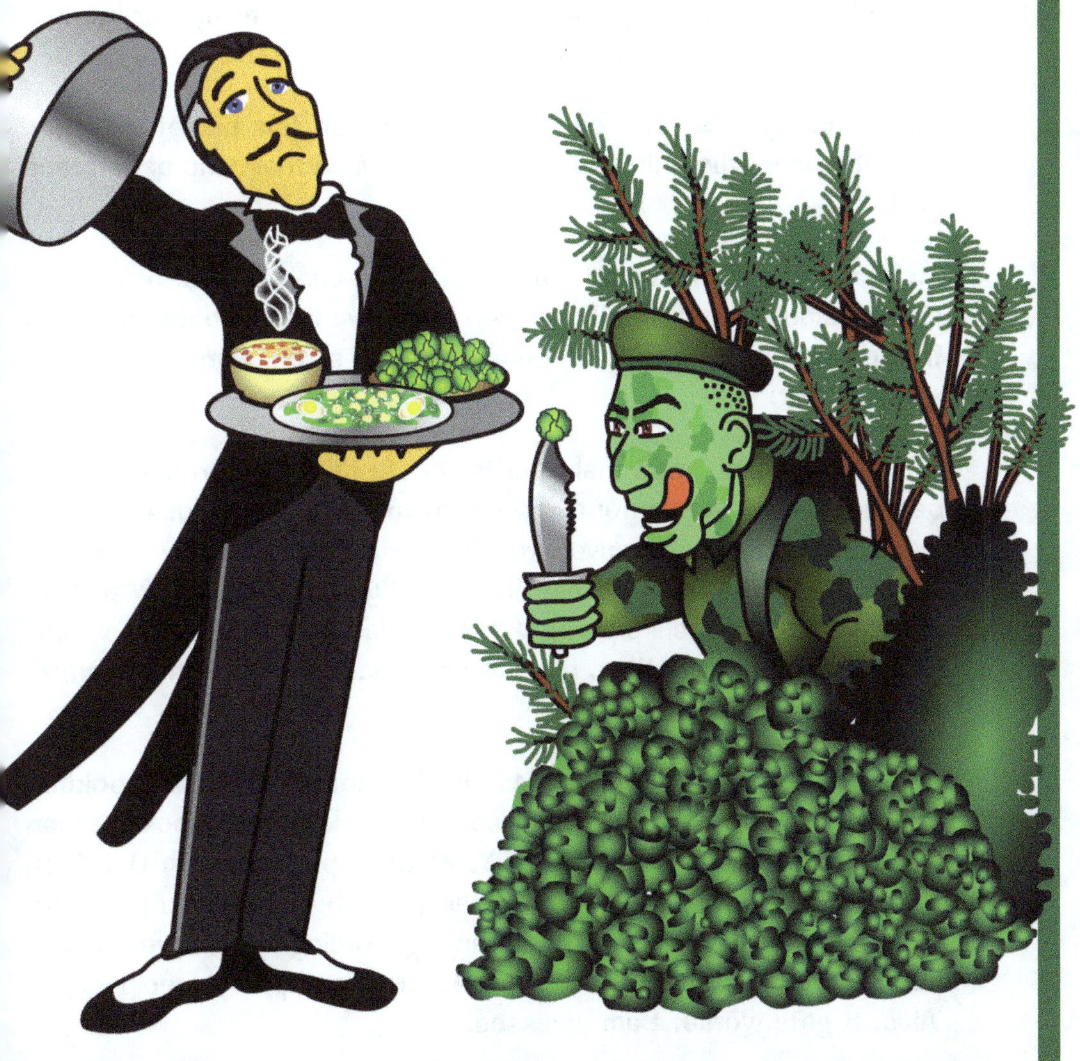

Something Sam Said

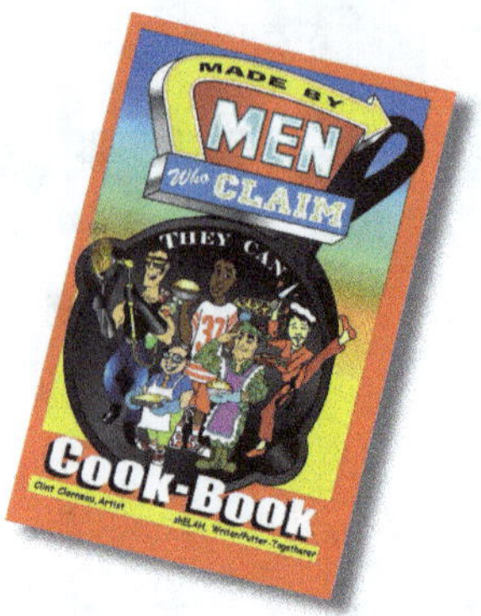

Women can't really cook, so consequently, men make better chefs than women. This reported "fact," brashly broadcast by Sam Holden, according to one reader, possesses the power to "stir up" or incite a full-fledged war between the sexes. Sam asserts that:

...The only people who can actually cook on this planet are men, even the ones who only cook once a year when their wife or girlfriend is ill.

...Men are often being told that we can't perform actions simultaneously, and that it's women who have these wonderful brains that enable them to walk and chew gum all at the same time. What absolute rot.

...[The fact that] men make better chefs than women is precisely because we are sensationally good at multi-tasking. For example, men can read maps and drive through any rush hour. Men can compute trigonometric equations while they are flying at Mach 2. Men can get roast beef, Yorkshire pudding, roast potatoes, cabbage and carrots all ready at the same time, and will have made their own horseradish sauce and "laid the table."

Sam argues that women will less likely experiment when cooking, while good cooks, "aka men," fearlessly take risks. When cooking, men "wonder whether X goes well with Y, or perhaps even with Q." They think that if their initial food formula fails, so what, they can just start all over again. Women, on the other hand, according to Sam, fear failure and consequently should stick to simple, tried and proven recipes.

Alas, it gets worse, Sam stresses...

9 Threatening Food Additives We Eat

1. **Partially Hydrogenated Oil:** Cuts manufactures' costs, stabilizes flavor, and increases shelf life, but a "lose-lose" for us. Difficult for our bodies to dissolve, but it boosts bad (LDL) cholesterol.

2. **High-Fructose Corn Syrup:** Highly processed form of glucose converts to fructose; cheaper than sugar shown to inhibit leptin—hormone that sends signal to your brain that you're full.

3. **MSG:** A chemoinducer of type II diabetes, obesity, and metabolic syndrome.

4. **BHA (Butylated Hydroxyanisole) and BHT (Butylated Hydroxytoluene):** Impact appetite and sleep, as well as contribute to behavioral problems, cancer, hair loss, kidney and liver damage.

5. **Sodium Nitrate and Sodium Nitrite:** Colorants preserve shelf life of bacon, hot dogs, sausage, etc. Mixed with stomach acids, they form nitrosamines, potent cancer-causing cells.

6. **Propyl Gallate:** Prevents fats and oils from spoiling, but often in conjunction with BHA and BHT, can cause cancer.

7. **Sodium Benzoate and Benzoic Acid:** Stymie growth of microorganisms in acidic foods, and when in beverages also containing ascorbic acid (aka vitamin C), can form small amounts of benzene; can cause leukemia and other cancers.

8. **Potassium Bromate**—Used to increase volume and produce fine crumb structure in breads/ rolls, it breaks down into inert bromide which may cause cancer.

9. **Food Colorings:** Red #3 demonstrated chromosomal damage and thyroid tumors. In lab testing, Red #40 spurred lymph tumors. Yellow #5 (aka tartrazine) and #6 may cause thyroid/kidney tumors, lymphocytic lymphomas, and chromosomal damage.

**O taste and see that the Lord is good:
blessed is the man that trusteth in him.**
~ Psalm 34:8

Johnny Cash's Chili

5 pounds sirloin steak
3 packages McCormick®,
Schilling®, Lawry's®, or any
   good chili seasoning mix
Mexene Chili Powder
Spice Island® Chili Con Carne Seasoning
Cumin
Thyme
Sage leaves

Chopped raw onions
Chopped chili peppers
3–4 cans red kidney beans
3–4 cans whole tomatoes
1 can tomato paste
garlic powder
onion powder
2 tablespoons sugar
Salt to taste

➢ Chop steak and cook until medium with a little shortening added. Add packages of chili seasoning mix and cook five minutes. Add beans, tomatoes, spices, raw onions, sugar and chili powder and/or chili con carne mix.

➢ Taste. If too hot for the children or ladies, add 1 or 2 cans of tomatoes. Add tomato paste. If it gets too thick, add water.

➢ Simmer low for 20 minutes.

Serve with soda crackers and Pepsi or Coke. This will feed 12 people 3 helpings each.
*You must guess at the amount to use. Do not measure them.

*Prior to giving this recipe to Mama Cash for her book, I never gave anyone the true ingredients. I have been known to substitute things like snake meat and such for the steak. This is the real recipe.

Oh that men would praise the Lord for his goodness, and for his wonderful works to the children of men! For he satisfieth the longing soul, and filleth the hungry soul with goodness.
~Psalm 107:8-9

Sherry's Country Cornbread

2 cups self-rising cornmeal

1/3 cup all-purpose flour

1 Tablespoon sugar

2 cups buttermilk

3 eggs, beaten

1 Tablespoon bacon drippings or vegetable oil

Second Step:

1 teaspoon oil for skillet

† Mix all ingredients together until well blended.

† Heat 1 teaspoon oil poured into cast iron skillet or corn sticks pan in 475° oven until hot; hot; hot but not smoking.

† Reduce oven temperature to 450°.

† Pour cornbread mixture into heated skillet or pan.

† Bake for 20–25 minutes.

† Yield 8–10 servings or may be used to make Cornbread Dressing.

Linda's Note:

Cornbread makes a better crust when it cooks fast in a super hot, cast iron skillet.

***Breece's Café Flavors of Centerville* Cookbook**

Available from:
**Remember When
108 S Public Square
Centerville, TN 37033**

Phone: (931) 729-0052

Sweet Potato Casserole

Ingredients

Sweet Potato Filling

3 pounds (about 4 medium) sweet potatoes or two large cans

½ stick (4 tablespoons) unsalted butter, melted

½ cup half and half

¼ cup maple syrup or honey

½ teaspoon vanilla extract

¼ teaspoon ground nutmeg

½ teaspoon fine salt

Pecan Topping

3 tablespoons unsalted butter, softened

¼ cup packed coconut sugar or dark brown sugar

¾ cup pecan halves or pieces, chopped

½ teaspoon ground cinnamon

Pinch of salt

Directions

Preheat the oven to 425 degrees F. Line a large, rimmed baking sheet with parchment paper . Grease a 9-inch square baker with butter.

To prepare the filling: Pierce each sweet potato with a fork or ice pick approximately five times to permit steam to escape. Place the whole sweet potatoes on baking sheet and bake until they easily squeeze (between 45 minutes to 1 hour 15 minutes). Set aside to cool.

Reduce oven temperature to 350 degrees. Once sweet potatoes cool enough to safely handle, slice each one in half. Use a large spoon to scoop insides into a large mixing bowl. Discard the skins.

Add the melted butter, milk, maple syrup or honey, vanilla, nutmeg and salt to the bowl. Use a hand mixer to whip the ingredients together until smooth and creamy (may use a potato masher or stir by hand). Scoop mixture into the prepared baker and spread it in an even layer.

To prepare topping: In a medium bowl, combine softened butter, sugar, pecans, optional rosemary, cinnamon and salt. Stir until the mixture blends. Dollop small forkfuls evenly all over the sweet potato filling.

Bake 30 minutes, until pecans become golden, and the filling sizzles around the edges. Serve warm or cooled.

Dis-Moi ce que tu manges, je te dirai ce que tu es

Dr. Scott Jutte

(Excerpt from forthcoming book, ***Better Health, Simple as THAT***)

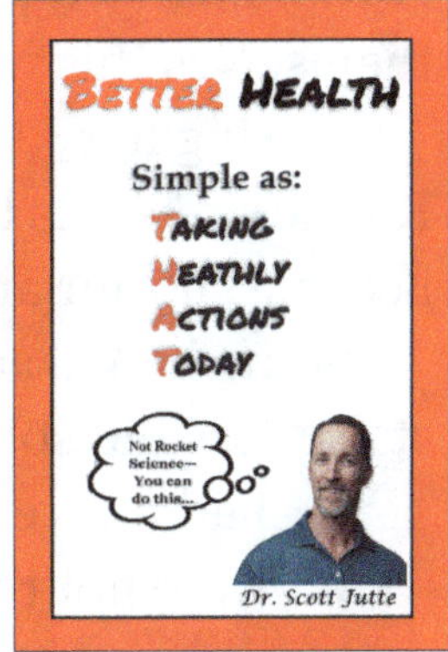

"You are what you eat." French lawyer Anthelme Brillat-Savarin coined this term in 1826 in"Physiologie du Gout, ou Meditations de Gastronomie Transcendante." It appears as: "Dis-Moi ce que tu manges, je te dirai ce que tu es. (Translation: Tell me what you eat, and I'll tell you what you are).

Despite America being one of the richest countries in the world, we eat too many foods that make us what we have become—poor in nutrition. As a result, what we eat tells the world that we are the most overweight, malnourished people on Earth. More than 50% of the world's 671 million obese live in the US and the following nine countries (ranked from the number of most obese people): China, India, Russia, Brazil, Mexico, Egypt, Germany, Pakistan, and Indonesia.

If not addressed, rising obesity could contribute to future life expectancy declining worldwide, due to preventable, increasing diet related illnesses. Why some people are perplexed about being sick and broken down is beyond me. They should expect nothing less from routinely putting junk food into their body.

Instead of eating a steady diet of junk food, consistently nurturing one's body with "functional food" can powerfully nurture our health. Functional food (working term) does not have legal status. However, research reveals that food may be functional if it beneficially affects one or more of the body's target functions beyond adequate nutritional effects. This practice proves relevant to improving one's state of health and well-being.

Similar to the way light overpowers darkness, better health from simple, natural, and functional foods contributes to reducing and/or eliminating risks of diseases.

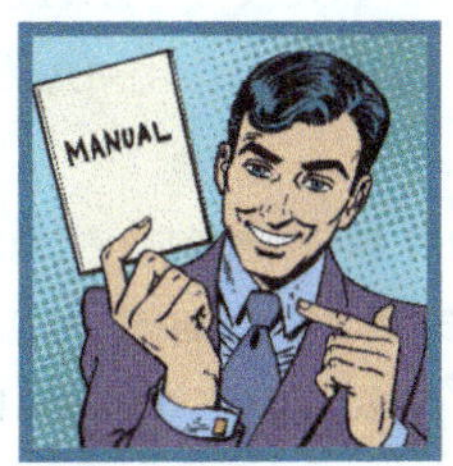

Celebrate Recovery... Jesus and Sobriety

"Hi, my name is Ruthie. I'm an alcoholic."

For years, while she stayed active in AA and tried to stay sober, Ruthie, as well as others attending meetings, had to introduce themselves this way: "Hi, my name is..."

During her 3½ years in AA, instead of staying sober, however, Ruthie's relapses became more frequent. The times she stayed sober became shorter and shorter.

Some in AA, according to Ruthie, claim that those who failed to stay clean and sober:

> had not yet hit rock bottom.

> were not ready.

> did not attend enough meetings.

> weren't doing step work [12 steps in AA program].

> had the wrong sponsor.

> will either be sobered up, locked up, or covered up.

Although she agreed with many of these previous statements, repeatedly introducing herself as an "alcoholic,"and repetitively relapsing, depressed her. She stopped going to AA meetings.

"Leaving AA and attending Celebrate Recovery (CR) turned out to be one of the smartest decisions I ever made," Ruthie said. "It took me removing myself completely from AA to stay sober. I learned the hard way that anything we put before our Lord and Savior, Jesus Christ, even AA, will become our master." Ruthie realizes she will either live up to or down to, whatever label she gives herself.

In Celebrate Recovery, Ruthie says with a smile, "Instead of focusing on our negative labels, we 'celebrate' our sobriety. Because of Jesus Christ, we can be free from our hurts, habits, and hang-ups."

Now, instead of citing and cringing at the words, "I'm an alcoholic," a clean, sober Ruthie regularly attends Celebrate Recovery meetings and proclaims "I am at peace. Today, I introduce myself as, 'Hi, I'm Ruthie and I'm a grateful believer in Jesus Christ.'"

**Do you not know that
to whom you present yourselves slaves to obey,
you are that one's slaves whom you obey....**

~ Romans 6:16a

What are You Waiting for?

Have you come to the place in your spiritual life where you know without a doubt that if you died today, you would go to Heaven?

If you answer "No," or have a doubt, and want the assurance of going to Heaven, I encourage you to pray the following prayer and do the best you can to mean it with all your heart.

Lord Jesus,

I know all have sinned, and that includes me. I ask You to forgive me, come into my heart, and save me.

I receive Your gift of eternal life. I know You died for me, and shed Your blood as a sacrifice for my sins on the cross.

I know now that I am saved, born again, and going to Heaven because of You, Jesus.

I believe with my heart, and confess with my mouth that Jesus Christ is my Lord and Personal Savior.

~ Amen.

Your name: ___________________________________

Date: __________ / __________ / __________

Time: _____:_____

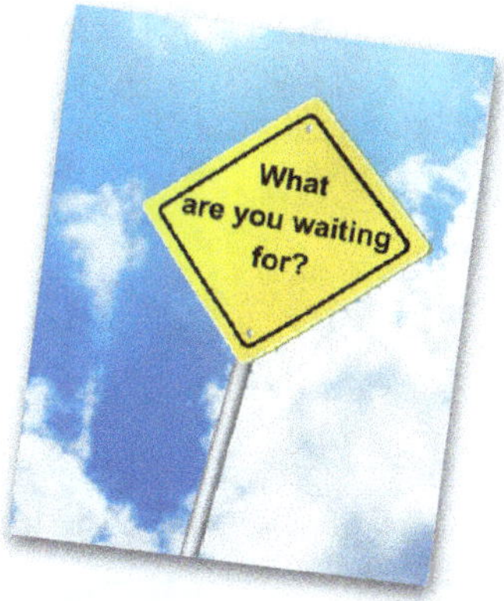

John B. Vennell, PhD.
Faith Community South Church
3115 Main Street
Cottondale, FL 32431

October 2022

Mon	Tue	Wed	Thu	Fri	Sat	Sun
					1	2
3	4	5	6	7	8	9
10	11	12	13	14	15	16
17	18	19	20	21	22	23
24	25	26	27	28	29	30
31						

November 2022

Mon	Tue	Wed	Thu	Fri	Sat	Sun
	1	2	3	4	5	6
7	8	9	10	11	12	13
14	15	16	17	18	19	20
21	22	23	24	25	26	27
28	29	30				

The National Banana Pudding Festival

Each year the first weekend in October, people near and far to Centerville, Tennessee, attend the National Banana Pudding Festival. Created to benefit local non-profit organizations and their missions, this festival has become the ultimate gathering for one of the South's best comfort foods.

A National Cook-Off for the Best Banana Pudding in America takes place along with live entertainment, arts, crafts, food, games and activities for the kids. As they support non-profit missions, those attending also get to sample dozens of different Banana Pudding recipes, and experience true Southern hospitality.

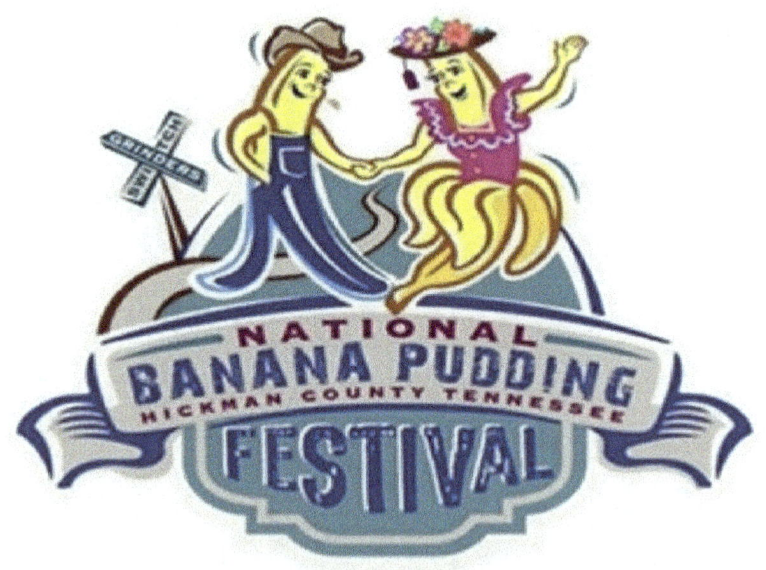

For more information, visit: www.bananapuddingfest.org

Phone: 931.994.NBPF (6273)

Mailing Address:
118 Church Street
Centerville, TN 37033

Festival Location:
Centerville River Park
104 Mary Field Ave.
Centerville, TN 37033

No... No... No—Not a "Nut"

No... no... no, according to Harvard Heart Health, a peanut *ain't* no "good for nuttin...," lowly nut. The name scientists gave the peanut "Arachis Hypogaea," which means "under the earth," stimulates a plateau of interest... *What?* regarding myriad of uses of this underground wonder legume.

Instead of qualifying as a "nut," a peanut, a legume like soybeans and lentils, with edible seeds inside pods, grows underground. Also known as the groundnut, a species in the legume "bean" family grows in Africa, South Central America, India, and Mexico.

Similar to tree nuts, peanuts offer rich, healthy unsaturated fats and fiber, as well as numerous vitamins and minerals. Several studies indicate that people who routinely eat peanuts or tree nuts have lower rates of heart disease than those who seldom eat them.

If you like peanut butter, but do not yet make your own, purchase a brand made of 100% peanuts with no added sugar or salt. Instead of topping peanut butter inside a sandwich with *sugarfied* jelly or jam, spread thin slices of an apple or a banana on it. Other ways to use peanuts, include drizzling peanut sauce on steamed broccoli or other vegetables; adding chopped, roasted peanuts to a stir-fry.

Or, no matter what you call the supercalifragilisticexpialidocious peanut, make a point to eat a handful of roasted or a cup of boiled Arachis Hypogaea regularly.

Yes... Yes...? Yes....!

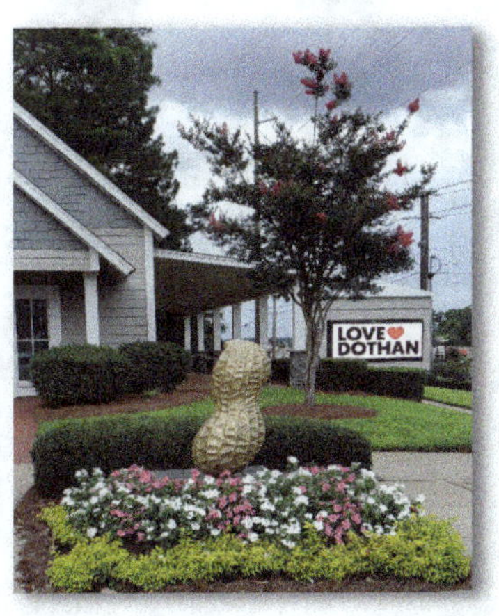

Each fall (November 4-13 in 2022), Dothan, Alabama hosts our country's largest peanut festival. The National Peanut Festival honors local peanut farmers and celebrates the harvest season. Dothan, known as the "Peanut Capital of the World," provides a prime location for growing peanuts. In February 2008, Colin Jackson (UK) set the record for the farthest peanut throwing distance: 37.92 meters (124 ft 4 in).

I went down into the garden of nuts...
~ Song of Solomon 6:11

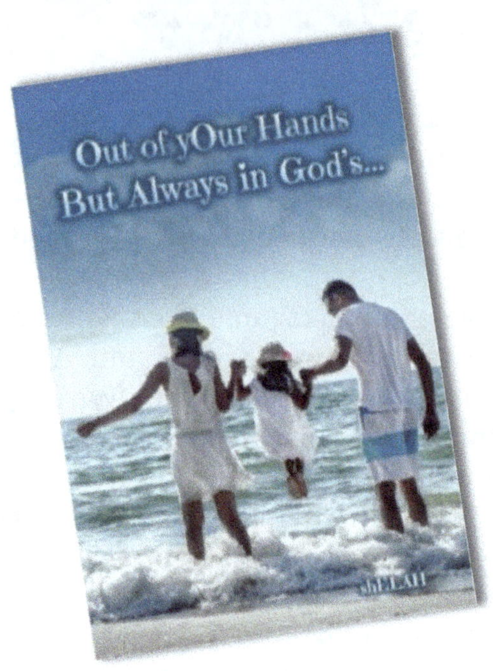

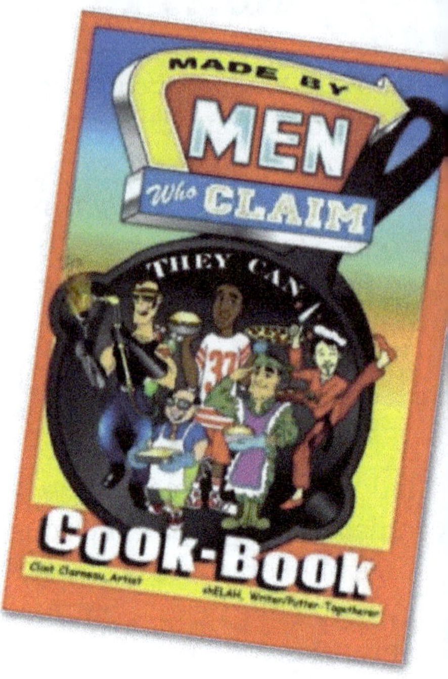

Books by yOur Backyard Publishing

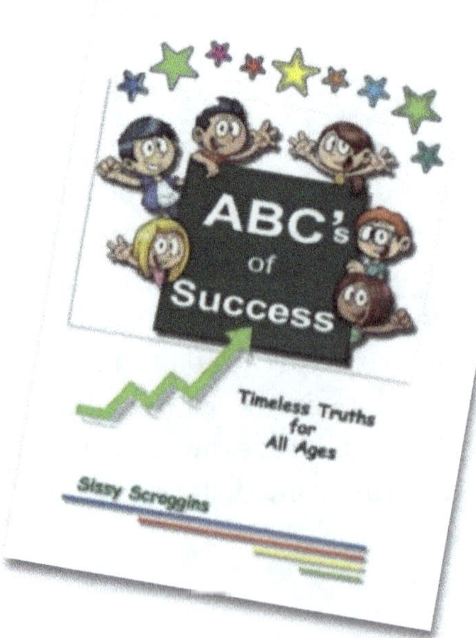

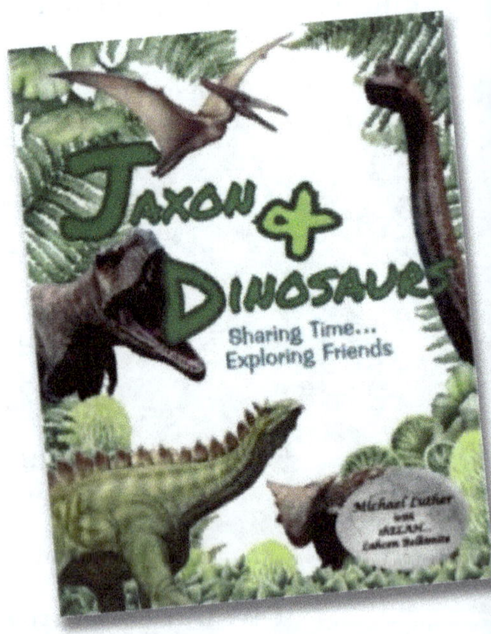

Sponsoring Opportunities

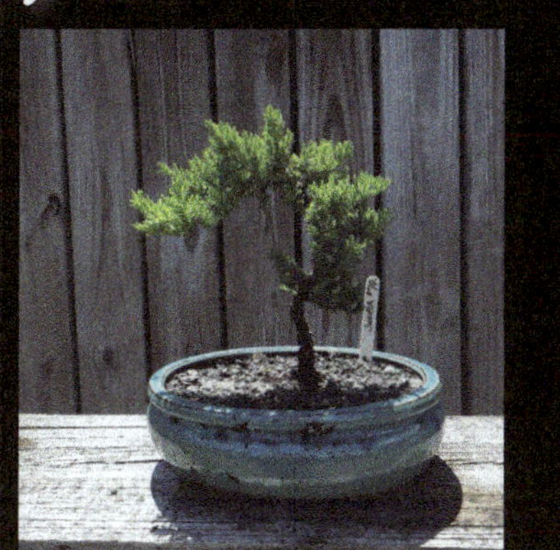

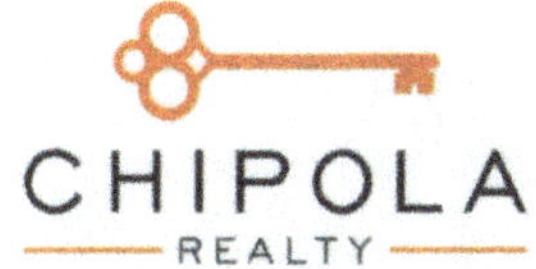

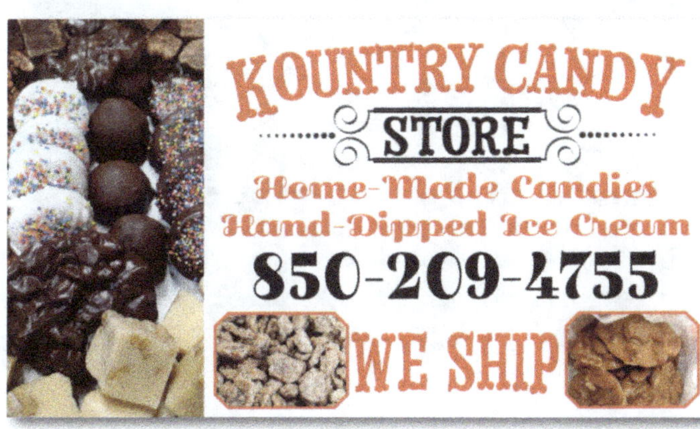

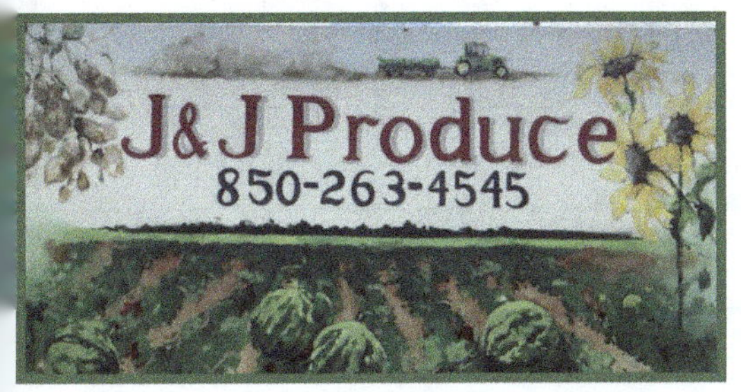
J & J Produce
850-263-4545

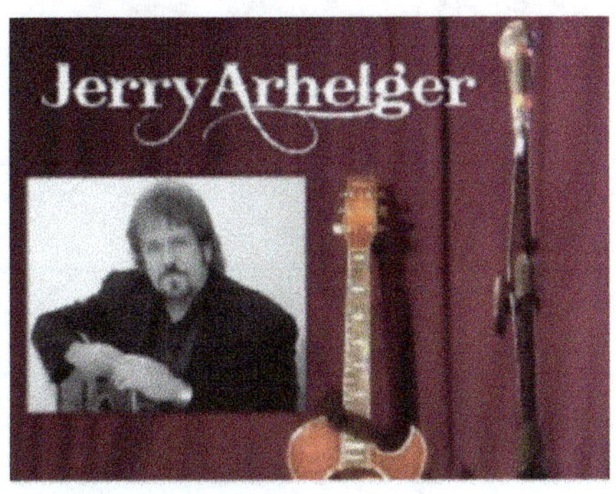
Jerry Arhelger

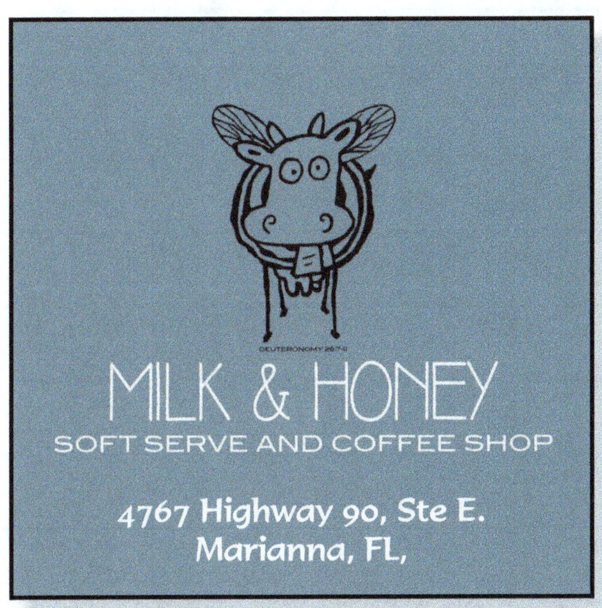
MILK & HONEY
SOFT SERVE AND COFFEE SHOP
4767 Highway 90, Ste E.
Marianna, FL,

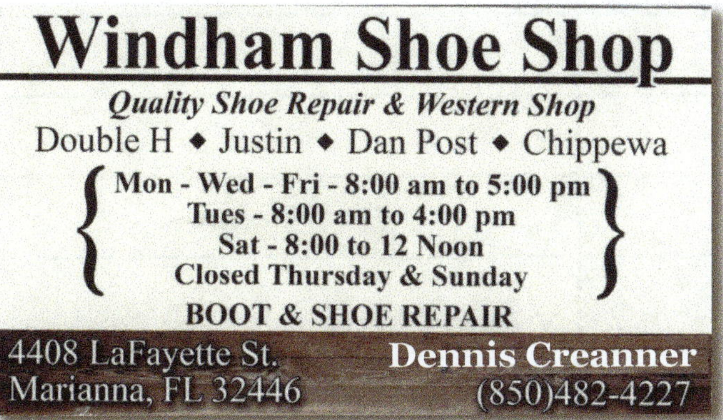
Windham Shoe Shop
Quality Shoe Repair & Western Shop
Double H ◆ Justin ◆ Dan Post ◆ Chippewa
Mon - Wed - Fri - 8:00 am to 5:00 pm
Tues - 8:00 am to 4:00 pm
Sat - 8:00 to 12 Noon
Closed Thursday & Sunday
BOOT & SHOE REPAIR
4408 LaFayette St.
Marianna, FL 32446
Dennis Creanner
(850)482-4227

www.ingramcontent.com/pod-product-compliance
Lightning Source LLC
Chambersburg PA
CBHW071639030726
47592CB00008B/2864